DATE DUE		

Growing Up Agreeably

Bonerate Childhood Observed

Harald Beyer Broch

University of Hawaii Press

Honolulu

© 1990 University of Hawaii Press
All Rights Reserved
Printed in the United States of America

96 95 94 93 92 90 5 4 3 2 1

Library of Congress Cataloging-in-Publication Data
Broch, Harald Beyer.
    Growing up agreeably : Bonerate childhood observed /
Harald Beyer Broch.
        p.   cm.
    Includes bibliographical references.
    ISBN 0–8248–1243–3
    1. Children—Indonesia—Bonerate Island. 2. Teenagers—
Indonesia—Bonerate Island. 3. Child rearing—Indonesia—
Bonerate Island. 4. Socialization—Case studies. 5. Bonerate
Island (Indonesia)—Social life and customs. I. Title.
GN635.I65B76   1990
305.23'09598'6—dc20   89–49006
                                CIP

University of Hawaii Press books are printed
on acid-free paper and meet the guidelines
for permanence and durability of the Council
on Library Resources.

TO MY MOTHER

Contents

Preface

This book is about children, socialization, and Miang Tuu, a tiny village on the remote island of Bonerate in Indonesia. More specifically, it focuses on the development of children from birth through infancy, childhood, and puberty to adolescence. My intentions are twofold. First, I want to describe what it is like to grow up in Miang Tuu; how children play; which tasks they are assigned by their parents; how they are reared and educated by peers, parents, and other adults; and what their hopes are for the future. In this context, my aim is to give an ethnographical account of Miang Tuu children. Second, it is my hope that this work will be useful to those who are interested in socialization processes in a cross-cultural context. Much of what we have been able to say about children in the past has been based on information gathered only from white middle-class Western children. If we refine our skills in locating and distinguishing psychological and cultural elements in socialization processes and then manage to account for the interconnections between these factors, we could gain new insight into child development. We cannot reach this broad understanding unless we know how children grow, develop, and are socialized in environments and cultures that differ from those where most of our research on children has been carried out.

Cultural perspectives on infancy and early childhood have not been a vital issue in recent research and teaching in anthropology or in child development. This unfortunate situation has developed because relatively few studies on children in non-Western societies and cross-cultural studies in socialization have been available. This situation cannot be altered overnight, but I hope that the present work will prove useful through its focus on how children are brought up in an Indonesian setting. This should, for instance, direct our attention toward old questions such as the importance of cultural versus biological and universal psychological bases for development. The best way to find out which parts of children's development are universal and which behavior elements are culturally conditioned is through cross-cultural comparison. Solving such fundamental problems has not been my objective. But I have located socialization themes that are important in research on child development. Not only have I described them in practice, but I have also emphasized their setting and context. As children grow older, they encounter an increasingly larger variety of social settings. Each setting has a typical scenario and cast of characters; each culture has a particular meaning and prescription for proper behavior. Children are socialized in terms of not only *how* they should behave, but also how they should behave *where*. One important way a culture socializes is in the setting it provides (Super and Harkness, 1982; Whiting, 1980). My own fascination has centered on the similarities and differences in how individuals' feelings and behavior evolve within a given cultural code and environment. In other words, the intricateness of the individual and his or her distinctive characteristics within the frames of similarity that we call cultural groups has continually captured my curiosity.

In the Norwegian anthropological milieu where I received my professional training, questions regarding the place of individuals and their differences within a culture have not been regarded as very interesting topics for serious research in anthropology. This work is to some degree a reaction to a tradition in which a major research goal has been to reduce the different organizational forms observed in the field to the basic processes that maintain and adapt these forms to their environment. In my opinion, these models do not reflect societies adequately. Although the models "work," they seem more logical than the cultures and societies they represent. Another objection to these models is that they mirror a false impression of homogeneity. Social change and modernization processes may well fit into such models, but investigations of individual diversity in behavior, thoughts, and goals are not regarded as important. Bonerate culture and social life in Miang Tuu could have been described and analyzed in general terms to underline culturally standardized behavior. But I am more concerned about individual variation within the culture and the evolution of this variation than about a model that may represent Bonerate culture per se, but not real persons.

This is not a book on socialization with the primary intention of establishing rules of recruitment to social organization or to throwing light on the Bonerate and Miang Tuu social structure.

Rather, I want to show some common features that the village setting imposes on all children who grow up there and on their socializers. At the same time, I want to demonstrate how even small differences among village households and even among siblings are
important to our understanding of what it is like to grow up in
Miang Tuu on Bonerate. I agree, of course, with the important
notion of common ways of conduct—that is, that rules of behavior and ideology can be used to define and localize cultural groups.
But during my stay on Bonerate I was far more puzzled and
impressed by variations in comportment than by expected similarities. It is important to understand the dynamics of intracultural
variation in behavior and cognitive work in order to increase our
understanding of cultural groups. Equally important is the search
for fruitful and empirically based ways to understand and predict
human behavior, cognition, and emotions. In cultural studies an
interest in individuals is by no means a new phenomenon. More
than fifty years ago, Saphir wrote that

> The true locus of culture is in the interactions of specific individuals
> and, on the subjective side, in the world of meanings which each one
> of these individuals may unconsciously abstract from his participation
> in these interactions. (Saphir, 1932, p. 239)

My education as a social anthropologist at the University of
Bergen in the early 1970s and later my work as curator at the Ethnographic Museum, University of Oslo, took place at two institu-
tions where British anthropology—as represented by Edmund
Leach, Max Gluckman, Raymond Firth and others, combined
with dogmatic "Barthianism"—defined which anthropological
issues were worthwhile to investigate or research. Psychological
anthropology was not regarded as a worthwhile field of research
in these circles. Yet the present study on Bonerate children and
socialization in Miang Tuu is heavily inspired and influenced by
psychological anthropology. This means that I have tried to add
insight to and make more sense of my data by adding psychological theory to social theory. Because I am interested in the relationship between sociocultural variables and psychological variables
and their reciprocal effects, the questions I raise differ from those I
would have dealt with had I been interested solely in social anthropological interpretation of the data. For example, I write about
weaning, the development of bowel and bladder control, attach-

ment behavior, and emotional expressions. When I analyze how children adapt to sex roles, I am not satisfied with locating and discussing available models and accompanying sanctions for behavior. Even in small societies, children have multiple models for conduct, and it is difficult to prevent everybody from copying an "unsuitable" model. Likewise, no social sanction can compel an individual to conform, although it may motivate him or her to do so. I emphasize this here as an explanation for why this work does not primarily deal with the constitution of social structure and organization. When studying children on Bonerate or elsewhere, it is natural to seek inspiration from psychological child-development research; it is in that field and not in social anthropology that scholars have worked most consistently on childrearing and development.

I have not considered it important or even desirable to use my material on Miang Tuu children to advocate a particular social or psychological theory or model. On the contrary, I have combined different theories and models to present and explain various aspects of the data. Throughout most of this work I use a conceptual framework based on a Barthian approach to the nature of social processes. The essence of this method is recognition of options available to people in interpersonal encounters (see Barth, 1966).

The present work is arranged according to a chronological model, based on the natural development and growth of humans within their society. It is hard to know what mechanisms have been at work to shape responses that are not apparent until much later and operate over a long period in the developmental lifespan of individuals.

I therefore begin in Chapter 1 by raising the rhetorical question: Who are the Miang Tuu children? How children and childhood are defined is discussed in both a general cross-cultural perspective and the more specific Bonerate context.

Chapters 2 and 3 describe infancy, babyhood, and the period of childhood. My goal here has been to locate features of what might be regarded as typical of a Miang Tuu way to socialize the youngest community members. I take it for granted that the setting for social interaction and many of the experiences of the young children during these formative years lay the foundation for personality development and culturally constituted modes of expression both on the individual and collective levels. These two chapters thus lay the foundation for the analysis and understanding of late childhood, early puberty, and adolescence, which are the themes for the two last chapters of the book. Chapters 4 and 5, in a sense, sum up and elaborate on Chapters 2 and 3. However, my position is that babyhood and early childhood are not responsible for all later expression of personality. The sociocultural setting, together with psychological factors and significant events, mold personality through the lifetime of all individuals.

This study is based on data gathered during a one-year period (1978) of anthropological fieldwork in Indonesia. Most of the time was spent in the village of Miang Tuu at Bonerate. The fieldwork was sponsored by Lembaga Ilmu Pengetahuan Indonesia (LIPI) and the Hasanuddin University (Udjung Pandang). Financial support was granted by Institutt for sammenlignende kulturforskning, Oslo, Norway, and the Scandinavian Institute of Asian Studies, Copenhagen, Denmark.

In Miang Tuu I stayed in the home of *ibu* and *bapak lingkung*.[1] They and their children made me feel very welcome. Living, sleeping, and eating together for almost a year with next to no privacy joined us quite closely together. *Ibu* and *bapak* helped me in every possible way. They provided me with a good home and became my best informants, guides, instructors, and teachers on Bonerate culture and societies. My debt to my hosts in Miang Tuu cannot possibly be repaid by mere acknowledgment. Although neither my hosts nor other Miang Tuu villagers can read books, I regard my publications on Bonerate as a tribute to the islanders. My hosts and other villagers in Miang Tuu expressed fascination with the thought that people in such faraway places as "Norbelgia"[2] and other European countries—and perhaps North America and Australia—should learn about Bonerate and Miang Tuu (many Bonerate people recognized that few of their fellow Indonesians knew about their island). It is my hope that they would recognize this study as their own if they could read it, and that it may constitute a resource for them tomorrow.

---

[1] I follow Bonerate custom by using *ibu* and *bapak lingkung* and not the more correct *ibu* and *bapak lingkungan*.

[2] Bonerate people had no knowledge about Norway, but insisted that the name of my homeland would be "Norbelgia" in the Indonesian language.

Besides my host family and the other villagers of Miang Tuu, many people helped me immensely through their kindness and knowledge. My thanks go to my colleagues and students at the Ethnographic Museum, University of Oslo, who so often had to listen to me talk about Miang Tuu children. Thanks are also due to the University of Oslo, which granted me eight months' leave of absence to work on this book at the University of California, San Diego, in the period from 1982 to 1983. In San Diego I benefited immensely from the stimulating milieu at the Department of Anthropology. I am especially grateful to Roy G. D'Andrade and Melford E. Spiro, who read an early draft of this study and offered many valuable comments and encouragement.

More recently the text has benefited from: thoughtful suggestions by Jan Petter Blom and Jan Brögger at the Institutes of Social Anthropology, University of Bergen and University of Trondheim in Norway. Thanks are also due to Harold Frank, who graciously worked to polish the language in most of this book. Ann Christine Eek has kindly reproduced the pictures for publication.

The Ethnographic Setting

The Island of Bonerate

Bonerate belongs to *Kabupaten* (district) Selayar in the province of South Sulawesi in Indonesia. Its total 1978 population of approximately 5,400 includes people of various origins and affiliations. The largest ethnic group is the Bonerate, who are regarded as the descendants of the original population on the island and early Butungese immigrants. They call themselves *Orang Bonerate* and are referred to by the same term by their neighbors (Broch, 1981, 1984, 1987).

Bonerate, which means *flat sands,* has two minor hills, the highest of which reaches less than 600 feet (approximately 167 meters) above sea level. The island, formed from corals, is almost circular in shape and is fringed by extensive reefs. The island extends over approximately 27 square miles (approximately 70 square kilometers). Bonerate lies in the middle of the Flores Sea at approximately 7 degrees south latitude and 121 degrees longitude. The soil is of poor quality and in most places is no more than 20 to 30 centimeters deep. In fields that have been cleared, seeds are sown between coral-lime stones that pierce the soil everywhere and cannot be removed. The Bonerate landscape is dominated by large areas of approximately 2-meter-high brush vegetation. There are also patches of parklike vegetation with grassland and scattered large trees. There are no rivers or creeks, and water is a scarce resource during the dry season (usually from June to November). Due to ocean breezes and the shallow soil, the island soon becomes arid when the rains stop. During the dry season the water is often brackish and poor in quality.

In the past a combination of trading, slaving, and piracy formed

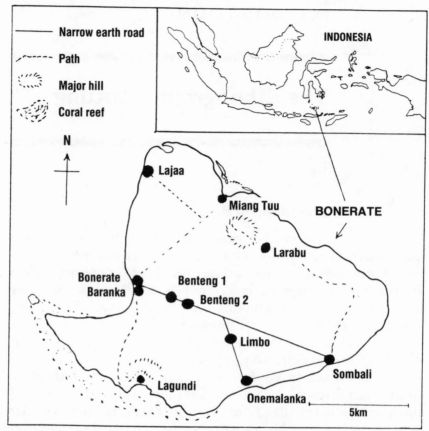

The Island of Bonerate

the base of the island economy, and the two latter activities continued well into the first half of the twentieth century (Jacobsen 1896, pp. 28–42; Kriebel 1920, p. 215; LeBar, 1972, p. 146). This background is important for understanding current resource management and the composition of social relations on Bonerate. Certain indicia point to the probability that the island was never able to feed a large population from domestic resources. Population pressures always seem to have been relieved somewhat by the customary period men spent at sea. Today most men of from sixteen to thirty years are absent from the island from six to ten months yearly, while they are at sea. This tradition improves the food situation for those who remain at home. Before they leave, the sailors take part in the labor-intensive work of the planting season; they are away during the critical months before the new crops can be harvested. As far back as people can recall, corn has been the staple crop, backed by some cassava and dry rice. Fishing has always been important for those who live in coastal villages, but the islanders regard themselves as agriculturalists and sailors, not as fishermen.

War dances and *joget* (a dance where girls and men dance together without touching each other) are popular entertainments in the largest village. However, only the descendants of nobles and other high-ranking people, such as civil servants and military personnel, may participate in these dances. In earlier times Bonerate had a stratified society with sharply defined classes: kings and queens and their descendants, nobility, commoners, and slaves. Today this social division is of almost no importance in everyday interaction.

Bonerate has ten villages; six villages are located close to the shore and three are inland.[1] The twin settlements of Baranka and Bonerate combined are locally referred to as *ibu kota,* the capital of the island (see map, opposite). Together they constitute the center of local Islamic, civil, and military administration. The island market is located here, as are a small health station and an elementary school. Although the island lacks a good harbor, the one situated at the local capital is among the best and can be used by small boats most of the year.

Although some fishing and agriculture go on, the major economic activity in Baranka and Bonerate is shipbuilding. The islanders build *perahu* of the *lambu* type, as well as modernized versions equipped with motors.[2] Baranka and Bonerate are the two largest villages on Bonerate island, and to the youth from the smaller villages, *ibu kota* seems fascinating, busy, and full of social life and entertaining possibilities.

In spite of the fact that most islanders consider themselves primarily agriculturalists, they are heavily dependent on the sea for

---

[1] The number of villages differs according to our definition. Lagundi, for instance, which is the oldest settlement on the island, had only twenty residents and may not be regarded a village. In Indonesia we also find a distinction between a *kampung* and *lingkungan;* here I equate *kampung* with *village.*

[2] *All ships built on Bonerate are made from wood, without nails. The lambu perahu is a sailing ship.* Those equipped with motors were bought by foreigners; no resident Bonerate islander owned a larger motor-powered ship in 1978.

protein. Most animal protein in their diet derives from fishing and gathering other marine animals such as worms and mollusks. In spite of the richness of the sea fauna, fishing is clearly second to agriculture in importance. The gathering of marine resources is generally done in what spare time is left after agricultural labor is completed—that is, at night or during the hottest hours of the day when the villagers find it too exhausting to work in the fields.

No game on the island is used and, being Muslims, the people do not breed pigs. The only sources of land animal protein are domesticated goats and poultry. Meat is distributed rather unevenly, however, and plays little role in the diet of most people. Bonerate hens are poor egg layers; thus eggs are scarce and not commonly eaten. People who live in the interior villages depend on trade and barter with members of the coastal communities for fresh fish, dried fish, and coconut oil, which is used almost daily in the preparation of food. Bonerate islanders practice a system of slash-and-burn agriculture. Due to the lack of water, only one crop per growing season is possible. Primary forest is nonexistent on Bonerate; secondary forest, in some instances, and bushland, in most cases, are cleared in the preparation of swiddens. Fields are usually cultivated for up to three years and then lie fallow from six to ten years. The technological level is low; a *parang* (long-bladed knife) and an iron rod for digging and weeding are the only agricultural implements in use.

According to official records, Bonerate is entirely Muslim. All villages have a mosque but, except during the month of Ramadan, they are poorly frequented. There are imams only in the largest villages. Elsewhere it is the privilege of the older men to read from the Koran; however, most of them do not understand Arabic and thus do not know the literal meaning of the texts they read. Traditional animistic beliefs are also an integral part of the religion of most Bonerate villagers. Offerings are presented at irregular intervals at small altars to provide good crops and good health and to thank spirits for good fortune. The altars, built of bamboo, form a simple grate that is hung by a tiny rope from a twig stuck into the ground. Altars are usually placed below large trees or on the beach facing the sea. The offerings are called *pakande,* which is the Bonerate term for food or a small meal. *Pakande* in this context consist of some boiled rice, one or two cigarettes, and water placed in a small bamboo tube attached to the grate. When offerings are made, a small fire is lit under the grate to make smoke sift through it. Beliefs in spirits are also demonstrated during various life crises such as at birth and at times of severe illness. On special occasions a possession-trance ritual is arranged (Broch, 1985a). Today this ritual also has many features of public entertain Bonerate religion is best characterized by what Casino defines as "folk Islam" (Casino, 1976, p. 94), a form of Islam that can be understood through examination of the people's own concepts of what constitutes Islam. These folk practices may well be quite different from "official Islam."

The Village of Miang Tuu

The village of Miang Tuu is situated approximately 5 kilometers from Baranka/Bonerate, the *ibu kota*. The road to Miang Tuu is no more than a narrow path winding through corn and cassava fields and patches of shrub. The village

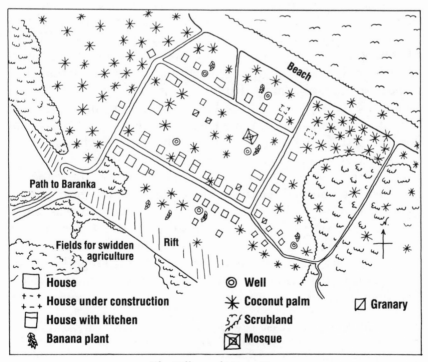

The Village of Miang Tuu

lies approximately 100 meters from a white, sandy beach. The houses are built on poles and made of locally obtainable materials, such as bamboo and rough wood. Mats of coconut palm leaves are used for thatching. The mosque is the only structure that uses sheets of corrugated iron on its roof.

At the end of my stay in the village, the 196 inhabitants lived in 46 houses occupied by 43 households. This represented a population increase of approximately ten times during the preceding thirty to forty years. The increase was to a large extent due to local immigration from other Bonerate villages. But there has been some immigration from neighboring islands as well; some people have come from as far away as Flores. No rules of endogamy or exogamy exist. Of the married population, some 50 percent moved to Miang Tuu at the time of their marriage. Less than half of the non-Bonerate immigrants are women. No Miang Tuu girl has married outside Bonerate or permanently left the island. This is consistent with an ideology of uxorilocality at marriage. When people marry, social prestige is at high risk. Bonerate people stress that fathers and mothers and siblings gain prestige through their daughters and sisters. Men try to move up the social ladder by marrying socially important or high-ranked women. According to what people say, a woman does not lose rank by marrying down. In 1978 bride-prices in Miang Tuu ranged from less than Rp. 20,000 to approximately Rp. 400,000.[3] Most weddings are arranged by the parents of the bride and groom, often with the assistance of the village headman and his wife. Wealthy parents of Bonerate girls find it natural to donate money to the family of the groom to enable them to pay a substantial bride-price.

Bonerate kinship is bilateral. The kin terms are the same for maternal and paternal relatives. There is a terminological emphasis on generation, and the island culture can be described as matrifocal (Broch, 1983). In everyday life the relative egalitarianism between the sexes, the cultural emphasis on mother–child ties, and the emotional focus on the maternal role are striking. Typically, authority is well distributed between husband and wife in a Miang Tuu household. To an outside observer, Bonerate mothers may

---

[3] Rp. rupiah. The Miang Tuu economy is basically one of subsistence and characterized by the absence of money in most transactions. Thus, both the amounts mentioned here are formidable to most villagers. When wages were occasionally paid for work, they ranged from Rp. 100 to Rp. 500 per day.

appear to be the major decision makers in both the house and village. The natives do not, however, concern themselves with the question of sex-specific dominance. On the individual level, there are dominating males as well as females, but social norms tend to eradicate such characteristics from public as well as domestic encounters. It is endemic to Bonerate culture that husband and wife are regarded as equals; they view the marriage union as one of cooperation.

Public village matters are topics of interest to all adult residents, and both men and women are heard. When ownership rights are discussed, women and men are involved equally because both women and men own property. Whereas some men may own boats and fishing gear, most married women own their house and household equipment; both men and women may own coconut palms and land rights. When disputes or other social and personal problems arise, male and female villagers seek advice from the village headman or *kepala lingkung* (more familiarly called *bapak lingkung*). In most instances *kepala* calls upon his wife *(ibu)* for help, and together they try to arrive at the best solutions. Matters brought before *kepala* and his wife may concern marriage partners, marital problems, finding spouses for sons and daughters, shortage of food or lack of money to pay tax, childrearing, locating work as a sailor, or the discontent of villagers due to the workload imposed on them by the *chamat* (district civil officer) in *ibu kota* or insults by people who disregard social rank and norms of conduct. Women sometimes seek out *ibu lingkung* for exclusive advice. When *kepala lingkung* and his wife are absent, people turn to any of the following villagers for advice: the oldest man in the village,[4] the assistant village headman, the daughter and son-in-law of *ibu* and *bapak lingkung,* and the husband and wife of one of the more affluent village households. Although I cannot rank these people by how often they are consulted, all have high social standing in Miang Tuu. They are relatively rich in material wealth[5] and are treated with respect and courtesy; they are always

---

[4] In Miang Tuu it is his privilege to read from the Koran when the context requires. He knows how to read Arabic although he does not understand the language. He is always offered the first serving at Miang Tuu feasts and other ritual occasions.

[5] Their wealth is demonstrated by their relatively large houses and their ownership of a *sampan* (small boat used for fishing), many coconut palms, household equipment, and *sarong*s, for instance.

served first and directed to the best seats wherever villagers congregate.[6] As for political and other issues that are decided on outside the village, neither the men nor the women of Miang Tuu have any say or much influence. Village life is usually monotonous, with hard work, few conflicts, and few festivities. The villagers do know about the outside world. Although several of the men have visited distant ports as sailors, Bonerate is in many respects a backward island, even on an Indonesian scale. Those living in the largest villages on Bonerate regard Miang Tuu as a remote location. The villagers have little interest in what happens at other places and communications are poor. In 1978, television had not reached the island and even radios were scarce in Miang Tuu; no one listened regularly to programs. Most villagers, especially children and youth, loved to listen to music, but there were usually no batteries for the radios and no money to buy new ones.

The Bonerate language, which is spoken in all villages on the island, is the language of local market communication. The reference to a Bonerate language is based on the islanders' own classification and the knowledge that the tongue spoken on the neighboring islands and Bonerate are not mutually understandable. This does not mean that the inhabitants of the different islands are always unable to communicate verbally. First, several Bonerate individuals master more than the local language, being bilingual and even trilingual. Second, a significant number of the islanders have some knowledge of *bahasa Indonesia* (the national language). Schools are being established on Bonerate, although not yet in Miang Tuu. Because most teaching is in *bahasa Indonesia,* this language will probably soon take over as the lingua franca.[7]

The economy of Miang Tuu villagers is a subsistence economy in which goods are produced or processed primarily for domestic consumption. The three comprehensive sectors of the Miang Tuu economy are swidden horticulture, fishing and gathering of other marine animals, and the sailing merchant *perahus* in the copra and spices trade between the Moluccas and Java. Pinpointing one sector as more important than the others is difficult because they are

---

[6] Courtesy in this context is very different from the servile behavior often observed when the villagers meet police, princes, and other notables.

[7] I was told in 1978 that there were no teachers on the island who could communicate in *bahasa Bonerate*. All the teachers were from other islands; some were married to Bonerate islanders.

thoroughly integrated. The villagers regard this question differently; they would without hesitation designate agriculture as their most important activity. Nevertheless, when fish are scarce or unobtainable in the village, people soon start to complain about the decline in the quality of life. We can only speculate as to why Miang Tuu villagers so rigidly present themselves as agriculturalists, while other Bonerate residents—for instance, those who stay in *ibu kota*—claim that Miang Tuu is indeed a fishing community. The reason may to some extent be of historical origin. Contemporary Bonerate islanders claim to have emigrated from agricultural areas on Butung five or six generations ago. Also, in the present Indonesian context, farming seems to have a status somewhat above fishing as an occupation.

Agriculture on Bonerate is generally the same all over the island. It is best characterized as established swidden farming in an integral shifting system (Conklin, 1957; Chin, 1977; Broch, 1985b). There is some variation in crop combination; for instance, some villages grow tobacco, others more bananas, and the inland villages have no coconut palms. Miang Tuuans do not depend on a single subsistence crop. Their horticulture is diversified, so that most contingencies can be met and overcome. The village fields are situated in an area that extends from the village site to a distance of approximately twenty minutes' walking time. There is no land shortage. A large variety of crops are grown in Miang Tuu, the most important being the staples, corn and cassava. Pumpkins are also important. In 1978, pumpkins served as staple food for more than thirty days when the stored corn was depleted in the village. The vegetables grown include peas, beans, peanuts, tomatoes, cucumbers, and watermelons, and small quantities of others. The season for various vegetables is quite short due to the shortage of water during the dry season. Irrigation has not been tried, and no fertilizers are used. The villagers know about the effects of urea but lack the money to buy fertilizers and pesticides.

The poor soil and the long dry season prevent extensive cultivation of fruits. Pineapple, for instance, is not grown at Bonerate. Some bananas are planted in and around Miang Tuu and *syrikaya* (*Annona squamosa*) are sown from seeds on the swiddens. Most years the yield is poor, and both bananas and papaya are regarded as luxury foods. In addition to banana plants planted at the wells to utilize water spilled when people wash, three lemon bushes, some papaya, and a few breadfruit trees grow in the village. These are all the property of different households. Large mango trees are found in most parts of the island. These trees and their fruits are common property of all islanders, and nobody remembers who planted them.

After corn and cassava, coconut palms are the most important plant. These palms are used in many ways: the leaves are used for roofing, the nutshells and coverage for fuel, the flowers sometimes for ritual purposes, and the shells as kitchen utensils. In many households grated coconut, mixed with cassava flour, is prepared daily at the end of the dry season; and coconut oil is an important ingredient in cooking. Coconut palms can be harvested at most times of the year, as the nuts are not seasonal.

Miang Tuu coconut palms are owned individually. All households do not own palms, but nuts are available to everyone, according to fixed harvesting rules.

The waters, lagoons, and reefs encircling Bonerate are open to all for fishing and gathering, regardless of birthplace or current village connection. The technological level of fishing, like that of agriculture, is remarkably low, although the villagers are exposed to the more advanced fishing gear utilized by fishermen from neighboring islands. Miang Tuu villagers use four basic fishing methods: (1) fishing with a baited hook and line, (2) fishing with traps, (3) fishing with nets,[8] and (4) fish hunting by rubber-string harpoon gun. Most villagers practice only one method; a few use two or more. Some households have no members who fish; however, all households are engaged in gathering. Animals such as bivalves, gastropods, sea urchins, and marine sandworms are gathered (see Broch 1985b for more detail on resource utilization).

Miang Tuu is a small village where all of the residents know each other well. It is a dense community where few secrets can be kept from fellow villagers. This setting provides a good feeling of unity, but also at times "a feeling of being watched and having to conform," the villagers say. Most Miang Tuuans express love for their home village, although young boys in particular sometimes say that they long to see foreign places. Miang Tuu appears to be a good and pleasant place to live.

---

[8] During my stay in Miang Tuu only two households owned gill nets, and these nets had small meshes, 2 centimeters by 2 centimeters.

CHAPTER I

The Miang Tuu Children

Too often we take the concept of childhood for granted, because wherever we encounter viable human societies there are children roaming about. Both laymen and social scientists speak about child cultures as cultural expressions existing in addition to or paralleling adult society. In the extreme, child cultures are viewed as isolated "social end products" transferred from one generation of children to new generations of children. These important cultural attributes seem of little use in their own right and of little relevance to the adults. Most people recognize their own childhood as important, but primarily childhood serves as a repository for the adult's memories from times past.

Another extreme view, held by a colleague of mine, is that there can be no legitimate reason for studying children as they will always be nothing but replicas of their fathers and mothers or—perhaps more generally—of their ancestors! In working to understand societies and cultural expressions, he explained, you would soon get totally lost unless you were studying the adults, who "know what culture is about."

I do not symphathize with either of these views. In spite of children's constant presence in a cultural setting, we cannot take much for granted about the character of their childhood without thorough investigations. In the first place we do not necessarily know who the children are! And this is not a question the youngsters can answer alone. Children are not living their lives in a social vacuum. Their adult relatives grant whatever privileges and duties their childhood is based upon. Economic, ecological, religious, and other cross-cultural factors will be relevant in reaching a culturally neutral definition of childhood. For instance, when children's work is needed in a particular mode of production, this fact will help define the situation of the children in such a culture, and what *we* may think of as a typical range of childhood activities could be significantly reduced. This implies that childhood is indeed a cultural construction. Who children are and how long individuals may remain children are matters determined by the adults. It is the adult members of the society who evaluate child activities as proper conduct for various developmental stages. The adult community grants its children permission to do certain tasks and prohibits them from doing others because parents and other adult community members share many goals for the children.

On the other hand, healthy children are seldom constrained by rules, norms, and parental goals and wishes to a degree that immobilizes them in complete obedience to all cultural demands. Rather, children tend to explore the boundaries of socially accepted behavior—either by cooperative testing of norms by peer groups or by individual experimentation. Thus, in most societies young children are soon taught that some norms have different relevance for different members of the community and they learn through experience that rights and duties are unevenly distributed even among the youngest household members. The following quotation should clarify the nature of the concept of childhood.

> A child is not solely a biological creature who comes to be influenced by the present-day socio-cultural circumstances of his birth. All children, because of the fact that they are born into a social environment, are affected by a construct that is peculiarly historical and, as such, has undergone many changes and reinterpretations in all societies. This construct is the concept of childhood that is used to interpret newborn *Homo sapiens* as children to the individuals responsible for their socialization. (Schwartzmann, 1978, p. 9)

Many societies of our time are characterized by torrents of modernization, sometimes leading toward a dramatic reorganizing of cultural arrangements. The problems experienced in those societies are fundamentally different from those experienced in the culturally more stable areas like Bonerate. Where cultural and social changes occur too fast, parents often show signs of severe frustration with not knowing "the best way" for their children's upbringing and education. The traditional ways may appear old-fashioned and of little relevance in the new world, but the adult community members often know no alternative means of livelihood. As children mature they too get caught by the social insecurity of their socializers. What is to become of the children? Parental goals may appear unrealistic, and the children themselves lack models to guide their way in an uncertain future.

Bonerate culture is by no means static, but so far changes have emerged gradually and with a speed that has permitted continued cultural integration. This is one of the reasons the study of Bonerate children is so fascinating. Here, both parents and children see few possibilities for the future that they cannot handle within their familiar cultural adaptation. This is particularly true of Miang Tuu residents who even by Bonerate islanders are seen as an isolated village community. The village has no school, and, even if Bonerate schools in theory were open to children from Miang Tuu, no villager made use of that opportunity during 1978. Some few children had previously attended classes at Bonerate, but they had dropped out. Thus, Miang Tuu provides a setting where formal education is almost absent, and the socialization of children rests on the community members alone.

Typically, all possible means for earning a livelihood at Bonerate, as this is understood by the villagers, are represented within the local community. There might be a few exceptions, where adults and children aspire to opportunities presently not realized in Miang Tuu—for instance, the running of tiny shops like those in the local *ibu kota*. To start such an enterprise is an expressed wish of both some adults and children. Otherwise, the villagers seem confident in the expectation that the children will follow the paths of contemporary resource utilization and general adaptation. During my stay in Miang Tuu I often spoke about these matters with both children and adults but never met individuals who expressed wishes beyond the village or intended to seek new ways to make a living. The only exception was a teenaged boy who told me that sometime in the future he wanted to travel to Bali, bringing with him a bunch of fierce fighting cocks to earn quick money in cockfights, and then to return to Bonerate, where he would erect a house of concrete. But he did not seem to have too much confidence in the project! His statement would have been regarded as childish by the adult community members.

That adults are supposed to keep emotions under firm control implies that spontaneous emotions are seldom expressed. This also implies that daydreaming or verbal and nonverbal expressions of flight from reality are publicly frowned upon. Emotional outbursts usually occur in situations of high tension and social friction or when spontaneity is ritually accepted.

Besides the obvious and easily observable traits of maturation from infant through toddler, young child, and older child to adolescent youth, Bonerate's way of defining children and childhood stresses the emotional development of the individual child. The Miang Tuu villagers place importance on the development of *individuals*. In addition to a common acceptance of both psychological and physical child development as gradual processes, my informants firmly stressed that each child has his or her own pace and peculiarities in growth from child to adult. Just as children vary greatly in the time they take to stop soiling or to learn to walk, they need different lengths of time to learn to control their emotions.

The Miang Tuuans are not much concerned about keeping precise track of the time. When children are older than two years it is hard to get their exact age from the parents. The date of birth is forgotten, to the extent it was ever noticed. Accounts of the age status of children are generally made with reference to social events, such as rites of circumcision and rites of marriage, and to an evaluation of emotional control in varying situations. I shall discuss the different rites of passage later and here merely point out that in Miang Tuu such rites do not mark a sharp break in most social routines of the novice. Even on these occasions the adult community admits that physical and emotional development do not necessarily follow each other.

Miang Tuu infants are not young children in the same sense that we consider babies to be in the Western world. Infants form a category of their own, characterized as a stage of transition. The newborn has its own kind of will and is extremely vulnerable to experiences of disruption and shock. The special "will power" of a Miang Tuu infant is not directed toward the community. It is rather an abstract impulse that judges the situation the baby child later will encounter in its household and evaluates the present means of nurturance and provisions available there. If the circumstances are not found to be proper the "will/soul" returns to the "universe" (the land of unborn). The observable result of this is the death of the infant.

According to the villagers the loss of an infant is not as hard for the parents as the loss of a baby. This conceptualization of the nature of postnatals may serve collectively to rationalize and reduce the guilt that might be felt by parents when infants die.

The transition from infant to baby, which is not observable to humans, starts at birth and normally takes from two to four months to complete. Thus, a 5-month-old baby is an emergent child ready to start on the long developmental journey to adulthood.

Typically Bonerate children are defined as being *bodoh* (stupid) —that is, they have no wisdom or knowledge of social norms and values. By implication they are not responsible for their misdeeds and behavior, and you cannot demand much from them. However, I was presented with some exceptions to this general statement. Some of the exceptions may be explained by the social status of the children and others by the fact that some activities are not affected by the ideology that the above statement reflects.

A characterization of children as *bodoh* also implies that they are emotionally unstable, more spontaneous in their social reactions than adults are. Expressing emotion in open aggression—for instance, in quarreling, nagging, or fistfighting—is considered a characteristic of childhood. Crying (with the exception of ritual crying) and overt and public demonstration of nurturant behavior, such as fondling animals and humans other than babies, are also childish acts. When children violate moral standards or cultural norms of conduct, they are excused with reference to the general fact that children are *bodoh*.

Just as Bonerate people cannot define precisely the onset of childhood, which comes after an introductory stage that lasts through infanthood and babyhood, they have difficulty describing the boundaries between childhood and adolescence and between adolescence and adulthood. These transitions are stages rather than fixed points. In most instances adulthood begins with marriage, but the full status of adult membership in the village is normally not granted until the first child is born to a couple.

Marriage age is approximately seventeen to twenty years for girls and nineteen to twenty-five years for boys; the time of marriage and the age of the partners, among other factors, are also related to the social position of the candidates. After marriage, individuals might still be *bodoh* on occasion, but this is stupidity of a different kind and not to be excused.

Severely ill people represent a cognitive problem for the villagers. When adults become ill they are treated like children. Sometimes they temporarily behave like children, losing self-control both emotionally (by being angry or short-tempered or acting self-destructively) and physically (by, for instance, losing control of bowel and bladder).

My informants could not decide whether sick adults merely acted childlike, or if they had temporarily regressed to childhood.

Miang Tuu people also believe that some individuals never mature to full adulthood. However, old men and women are not "children of old age"; they have vast life experience and wisdom that children never possess.

The Newborn Child

I still remember well the time when my first child was born. We were lucky; he was a strong boy child, Ali. I was so happy. When we found him a name and it proved to be a good choice, this was a name to me and my wife too. In a way we were like new members of the village.

After having had the first glimpse of my son, I had to run out of the house. There were too strong feelings inside me. I felt like running as fast as I could to my field and working really hard. Happy, I swung my *parang* and it flew through the air, cutting down brush and thorny bushes on its way.

But all of a sudden I got nervous and could not concentrate on my task. I had to hurry home to get it all confirmed. Could it all be true? And when I entered the village I heard the shrill sound of an infant crying from our house. What is wrong now? I thought. All pale and shivering, I climbed up and went inside, but there everything was well with both child and mother.

Like this the days went by. I did not manage to get much work done. Once out in the fields I became restless and wanted to return home to see my boychild, to hold him close. Then at home I was too restless to sit down; I felt I should return to the field and clear lots of land to provide enough food for all three of us.

Actually we have been just as happy because of every child we have been offered—but still, you know, only one is the first!

When it is a dark night like this and there is a newborn child in the house, we light a fire at the entrance to protect the newborn. Thus, we are also able to detect everyone who wants to visit. Some villagers fix thorny branches above the entrance or they place them at the threshold.

These utterances by one of my male informants are remarkable for two reasons. First, the events described are not representative; not all fathers are in the village when their firstborn child arrives. A significant number of new fathers are absent because they are engaged in the *perahu* sea trade between the Moluccas and Java. Thus, many fathers feel that they are strangers to their young children. This feeling is so common that the villagers often talk about it, especially when the return of the *perahus* is expected shortly. The life cycle is such that most men will be present at the time of the birth of some of their children, but usually not of the firstborn (Broch, 1983, p. 155).

Second, Bonerate people, women as well as men, rarely express their emotions either in words or in action. This informant describes the birth of his firstborn in a highly emotional way. Because I know him well, I can be certain that he does not habitually express himself with emotion. Other adults, both men and women, show far more emotional concern and behavior toward young children than they do in all other situations of social interaction; and the new father's statement is a strong indication of how important, both socially and emotionally, the births of one's own children are. Affection was most frequently demonstrated toward children, and only rarely were other social relations underlined as openly. This observation points out the warm feelings parents have for their young children.

Let us now take a closer look at the relationship of the father and the newborn child. Bonerate people claim they have no preference for the sex of their children, but if they have more than one offspring they say that the best thing is to have some of both sexes. In other words, both girls and boys are equally desired. Still "*bapak* Ali" or Ali's father stressed that when a name was selected for their firstborn son, this was also a name of reference for both mother and father. Thus, from that moment they would be called *ibu* and *bapak* Ali by most villagers in both reference and address. This custom of teknonymy makes the arrival of the first son a special occasion and especially so for the father. It is only after the naming of the oldest boy child that the parents themselves are also given new names of reference, unless or until this boy dies. If that happens, people cease to call the parents by father and mother of the dead child and instead apply the name of the eldest surviving boy. The names of deceased children are never mentioned, nor is the dead child talked about. In contrast, the names of adult members of the society are not tabooed after their owners' deaths; but only those who performed some unusual task or behaved extraordinarily are generally talked about. In Miang Tuu addressing a mother by *ibu* and her son's name is a sign of formality, but—although villagers agree that it would be proper naming—this use is not general. After the first son is born, the mother is still usually referred to and addressed by her maiden name. This would be her childhood name, or the first name. In Miang Tuu surnames are not applied or remembered, because surnames were only recently introduced by the civil authorities. For the father, however, only the most intimate friends and relatives would insist on continued application of his "old name."

This custom of naming parents could indicate a preference for boy children, but that would be a misinterpretation. There are no reasons to doubt the villagers when they express their preference for children of both sexes. Even if it is true that the birth of a girl does not affect the naming of her parents, a girl child brings so many hopes and expectations for the future of the household that she is indeed welcome. In Miang Tuu people say that it is just as sad to have no daughters as it is to have no sons! That this is more than just a saying will appear clearly when we see how complementarity between the genders emerges through childhood and adolescence.

Bapak Ali demonstrates through the description of his own emotions that he is concerned about the welfare of the infant. In a sense we can assume that the birth gave added meaning to his life and also marked the beginning of a new epoch for the household. Even the added workload and responsibility are not seen as negative. Under normal circumstances husband and wife do much work together, both around the house and in the fields. Now he is alone with many tasks but expresses joy about the fulfilling of his wife's and his own shared goal, which also automatically grants them full recognition as adult members of their society. Soon he and his wife would together accomplish their major task as husband and wife—namely, raising a family.

His dilemma was expressed with a smile: he could not stay close enough to the newborn child and at the same time provide the necessary food to support the family.

The Time of Pregnancy

Both newlyweds and well-established couples express a desire for children. Birth control of any kind is out of the question, as it is a truism that no parents can expect to see all their children reach maturity. The reality experienced is that more than 60 percent of all children born in Miang Tuu die before the age of three. According to what people say, the death risk is highest during the first three or four months. This grim fact may be reflected in the attitude toward infants. The major goal of their parents during the first years is to keep them alive; the demands of enculturation are low.

There is nothing supernatural and mysterious connected with the idea of conception and the resultant gestation period. Both are regarded as natural and normal events. Pregnancy is expected within a year or so after marriage. If this does not occur, the spouses are pitied. In this instance the young woman would normally be held responsible for their infertility, although the villagers do know about male sterility—for instance, due to diseases acquired from "bad" women in the harbors of Java and the Moluccas.

However, after a child is born to a couple, the failure to produce other children is always blamed on lack of virility in the male. This often leads men to be afraid for and much concerned about their potency, as they say that strong men are capable of fathering many children (see Broch, 1983).

When pregnancy gradually becomes more and more visible, social attitudes towards the expectant mother change. It is expected that the working capacity of pregnant women is reduced. When the woman gets heavy, she is regarded as unfit to work under the burning sun in the fields or to gather food along the beach. The rationale is that the hot sun, frequent bending, and rapid movements are not good for the mother and fetus.

As the time of delivery draws near, the pregnant woman keeps close to the house, often resting in the shade. Her husband and her parents or parents-in-law, if they live in the same village, try to help her in her daily chores. She is seldom left alone and is often seen amid other women chatting. The villagers claim that the expectant mother tends to be in an unstable mood at this stage. Her lessened self-control, for instance, is demonstrated by an unusually high level of irritability.

Somewhat more fuss is made about a first pregnancy than about those that follow. But late pregnancies to some degree also cause anxiety, as giving birth is always regarded as painful and hazardous to both mother and infant.

When there are other young children in the household, precautions are taken to help the youngest child adjust to the new situation and an altered status within the core family. Miang Tuu parents accept temper tantrums and other signs of a mild fear of separation as normal expressions of envy and maladjustment that are likely to appear in the deportment of the infant's brother or sister who is closest in age. Weaning is often late, and attachment to mother and other child tenders can be strong. A too-abrupt disruption of integrated habits and the feeling of safety is regarded as too hard on toddlers and young children. They are not expected to have developed an adult sense of rationality and mature understanding of the processes of life development.

Kartini, a girl approximately ten months old, showed signs of attachment behavior both to her mother and aunt (attachment and attachment behavior will be discussed in Chapter 2). The aunt, herself no more than ten years old, showed much childish affection for Kartini. She had major responsibilities for the daily care of her niece. Then the young aunt, together with her mother, father, and brother, left the village for Surabaya and did not return until a month later. This meant that Kartini not only lost her caretaker, but also her maternal grandparents who usually fondled her daily when at home.

A six- or seven-year-old substitute baby tender, Yobaida, was called for. She was made to understand that from now on she was responsible for the well-being and comfort of Kartini when the toddler's mother was out of sight. Yobaida spent most of her day in Kartini's company, carrying her on her hip, playing with her, kissing and hugging her, and depositing her close by when she played with her own age-mates. Some nights Yobaida slept next to Kartini in Kartini's home.

But when Kartini was left alone for a brief moment, she began crying almost instantly. According to her mother's interpretation of the child's behavior, she was missing her aunt. Gradually Kartini seemed to forget about her aunt; she seldom cried and did not panic when left a moment alone.

When the aunt one day returned to the village, Kartini clung to her and showed much exitement. But after a while she returned to Yobaida.

It was at this time that I observed that Kartini's mother was again pregnant. I wondered why Yobaida still was kept as baby tender when Kartini's relatives had returned from their voyage. I also noticed that Yobaida continued to sleep many a night by Kartini's side. The reason for all this was told without hesitation. Because Kartini would soon (in three to four months) have a new brother or sister, she would have to become gradually accustomed to not being the focal point of her immediate family. "It is always so; even if we love all our children, there will be much fuss about the newborn." Kartini's aunt would definitely focus her attention on the infant and wish to tend it as soon as possible. The mother would of course also be busy with the infant; the best solution was to have a nurse for Kartini from outside the immediate family circle, I was told. This example may not show how it is always done in Miang Tuu when children are born in close succession within a household, but this case demonstrates how many villagers would have made arrangements in a similar situation, if it had been possible. Yobaida and her mother were given compensation for the the little girl's work, but very few villagers were in a position to hire any help for extended periods of time.

When the time comes for a woman to give birth, her husband or other close relatives summon a midwife. The midwife might be the mother of the woman in labor or another trusted relative. The midwife is always a woman reputed for her various ritual skills and knowledge of delivery. In Miang Tuu there were four women who were often summoned to help at births. Parturition takes place in the most private part of the house. If it is a one-room house, a section is enclosed by a temporary curtain. The woman in labor is placed on a new sleeping mat on the floor, attended by the midwife and the mother (if she is not the midwife) and a sister or a best friend.

As Flores also reports from the Sulu archipelago (Flores, 1967, p. 85), Miang Tuu men in general stay away from a delivering woman out of modesty, unless their physical strength or knowledge of magic is required to facilitate childbirth. Miang Tuu fathers recalled that they had been nervous and restless when their wives were in labor. Giving birth is accepted as being painful, and the women are in no way constrained to behave bravely and silently. That the villagers are visually barred from the scene of birth does not mean that birth is not an important village event. Besides the fact that walls and floors of homes are far from soundproof, some of the women attending step outside every now and then to inform everyone about the progress of the birth. To keep his emotion under control, the husband walks about and chats with everybody, he often takes on the duty of making sure there is hot water ready for the midwife to wash the infant and the mother. As soon as the child is born, the midwife cuts the umbilical cord a few centimeters from the body with a fresh bamboo knife. She also ties it with a piece of sewing thread. After the umbilical cord is cut and the baby is bathed in boiled, lukewarm water, it is wrapped in a soft *sarong* and then put beside the mother. Before the new mother is urged to sleep, she is offered some broth made from rice.

As it has been reported from the Batek, childbirth is characteristically not highly ritualized. "Their procedures are addressed mainly to the practical problems of bringing babies safely into the world" (Endicott, 1979, p. 101). Yet without participating in any ritual, both the father and mother achieve a change of status as marked by their altered names of reference. The childbirth procedure is essentially the same whether it is a woman's first or tenth child, though there is no marked change of social status after a second girl or boy is born.

The use of medicines and spells can of course be considered ritual, but these are few, and the people claim that they are gradually vanishing from common practice. Yet in most households with a newborn child, a torch or small fire is lit to protect the infant after sunset. "Thus we are also able to see everyone who wants to enter," one male informant told me. Some villagers also attach thorny brush above the entrance or deposit them at the threshold. When both the mother and child are judged to be in fair health, usually after a couple of days, the midwife returns to her own home; if anything unexpected happens, she is immediately summoned. A midwife is regarded as close to all the children she has helped enter the world. If possible, she will always be called upon when people she received at birth get sick later in life.

After giving birth, women are weak and need to sleep a lot and rest. They do not resume work outside the house before three weeks have passed. During this time they remain inside the house most of the time. They are seldom left alone, as villagers of both sexes and all ages drop in to visit and to take a look at the child.

During the first week, mother and child wash inside using lukewarm water, often assisted by female relatives or friends. When the first week has passed without any complications, the mother returns to one of the village wells for her two daily baths. Dressed in her *sarong,* which is fastened below her armpits, she pours cold water over herself. The child may still be washed inside for some time, but now in ordinary cool well water. Before long the baby will join the mother at the outdoor bath. The mother holds the baby firmly against her own body while pouring water over them both at the same time. During the day the mother mostly cares for the infant alone. But until she can produce "adequate" quantities of milk, a wet nurse periodically nurses the baby; if no wet nurse is available, a broth made from rice is fed to the child. No milk other than mother's milk is available in Miang Tuu. Infants or children are never fed any kind of condensed or powdered milk.

At night the father keeps an eye on the child, picking up a crying infant to comfort it. If the husband is at sea, which is a common situation when the first child of a couple is born, company is always arranged for the mother and child during the night.

The child is handled gently, is fed when it wishes, day or night, and when crying, will usually be fed. Although pacifiers or similar substitutes are not used to comfort a child, occasionally women will pick up and calm a crying infant by letting the infant suck their dry nipples. The infant is not named at any particular time nor is the naming event ritually marked. The Miang Tuu villagers claim that a newborn infant really is not yet quite a human being. The body merely houses a "soul" that makes various inspections of the environment into which the child would be introduced. This "inspection" lasts about four weeks. During this time the soul is easily disturbed and offended. It has its own will and ways and will immediately depart if insulted. It is sad when the soul leaves the infant, because there will be no child, but the grief is easier to bear than when a child dies.

After the first four weeks have passed, the parents will search for a suitable temporary name. Without much fuss the infant is presented with the name and will be called by it for an undefined period of time. The parents are constantly on the alert, trying to make sense of the baby's signaling behavior. "Crying, smiling and babbling, and later calling and certain gestures are readily classifiable as social signals and have as a predictable outcome increased proximity of mother to child" (Bowlby, 1972, p. 297). The father and other relatives of the infant also pay much attention to its signals of communication.

> Nevertheless the circumstances in which each kind of signal is emitted and the effects each has on the different components of maternal behaviour are very different. Even a single form of signalling behaviour, crying, is of several different kinds, each kind being elicited by a different set of conditions and having a rather different effect from the others. (Bowlby, 1972, p. 297)

Bowlby's observations and discussions are relevant and interesting, but they also show how communication between infant and its social milieu is culturally defined, even at this very early stage. We may assume that the needs of infants are indeed comparable across cultures, even though the interpretation of their signals differ. Bowlby, for instance, identifies two categories of cries: crying from hunger and crying from pain. This is also in accord with Euro-American cognition. From other cultures, as for instance in Colombia, there is reportedly only one interpretation of an infant's cry—namely, as a sign of hunger (Dussán de Reichel, 1979). It is fairly commonly reported from various cultures that babies are fed whenever they cry.

Once a name has been found for the newborn in Miang Tuu, communication between infant and its mother and father becomes extremely crucial. The infant is now approaching humanity. Still the infant is fragile and if insulted may easily refuse to live. However, the baby owns a body of specific knowledge not shared by its parents. That is why the baby is given only a temporary name. If the name does not suit the infant for some reason, such as taboos unknown to the parents, the baby will try to signal this. If the parents fail to understand, the baby might refuse to stay alive.

Thus an infant's cry is in most instances regarded as a cry for food, but it might also indicate that it is dissatisfied with the proposed name. The villagers say it is difficult to interpret the signals a baby wants to give in these matters. But a baby that continues to cry after being fed several times, might be communicating an inappropriate naming. Also if the child shows other signs of dissatisfaction besides continuous crying, it is likely that it is urging a change of name. When the parents feel their chosen name does not suit the infant, they try another name and make sure the baby gets to know the new name. If an infant is happy with the chosen name and thrives, no alternative name is sought. Repeated babbling and smiling indicate that a right name has been found.

This period of trial for a suitable name may last as long as five months. If the baby after that time still is uncomfortable, this is most likely due to other reasons than a badly chosen name; the reasons may be hunger, physical pain and illness, or lack of company.

During the first three to four months, the infant is within reach of its mother most of the time, but the father and other relatives also hold the infant for shorter periods. The mother usually does not leave the village and does not return to hard agricultural labor before four months have passed.

The infant is fed on demand day and night, with no attempt to maintain regularity. Babies sleep with their mothers at least as long as they are regularly breast fed. They are never left alone but are either carried along wherever the mothers go or left in the care of their fathers for limited periods of time. An infant is considered completely dependent on continuous care, and every effort is made to avoid offending the infant.

Soon the day and the month in which it was born are forgotten. The parents of a child older than three years are never able to tell when it was born and thus have great difficulty telling the exact age. But the majority of the villagers keep track of the time only by referring to the market days at Baranka/Bonerate. They do not count days, months, or years.

Infants and babies are not held responsible for any misdeeds. As we have seen, the knowledge possessed by infants is of a highly specialized kind. Although they can recognize an appropriate name and are sensitive to insult, they do not know anything about decent behavior. On this Miang Tuu parents are quite explicit. Babies and young children have no knowledge whatsoever; they must learn everything from scratch. But there is no urgency in most matters of cultural education, and children who still do not know are not responsible for their behavior nor should they be punished for the violation of social norms of the adult population. At Bonerate most forms of development are regarded as taking place gradually. So also is the unmarked transition from infant fragility to early childhood.

When the baby is approximately four months old, the mother usually resumes her normal routines: working at the swiddens; collecting various molluscs, worms, and bivalves on the littoral zone; and preparing coconut oil. She will bring the child with her for many of her activities, but the situation of the baby is changing. Many new people enter its life to play important roles. Typically the child develops attachments to people other than the mother figure. The human status of the infant is confirmed and the mystical fragility disappears.

CHAPTER 2

Infancy and the Early Years

To describe and analyze Miang Tuu childhood, we can distinguish three phases in Bonerate child development. These phases do not correspond to a native model perceived by the villagers; indeed, such a scheme would violate their idea of a gradual process of maturation from infant to adult status. In accordance with the native model of child development, the three phases described here are not clearly separate but are to some degree overlapping.

The first phase, *infancy and the early years,* starts when the infant has been named properly. This phase typically covers weaning and toilet training, development of motor movement and speech; it lasts through the period when the child is regularly tended by various caretakers.

Childhood, the second phase, starts at an approximate age of five years. In this stage the world becomes wider, for children are free to roam about. At this phase youngsters also get their first assigned chores, such as carrying water and taking care of younger children. This is also the period when play activities dominate much of the child's time. At the same time tentative, informal instruction begins to be offered by adult villagers.

Late childhood and early puberty, the third phase, starts about the time of circumcision. Today physiological puberty sets in somewhat earlier than the social ritual display for the boys (see circumcision rituals, Chapter 4). At this time interaction between boys and girls is beginning to be more formalized. Both are more involved in various household chores such as agricultural work, fishing, and cooking. By now youths should also have developed a more formal understanding of social positions within the community. They become more attentive to their physical appearance and may often appear shy in situations where they were previously unconcerned.

In Miang Tuu, as in most other places, there are often large gaps between sociocultural generalizations and ideology on the one hand and actual behavior on the other. When mothers and fathers are asked about how they rear their children, they tend to answer the questions not according to what they actually do, but rather what they would have done in what they regard as an optimal situation. This response is again related to the structure of social position and rank within the village. Formerly Bonerate was a stratified society. The population of the island was divided into four strata: royalty, nobility, commoners, and slaves. Today these social distinctions have been officially abandoned; however, people know well from which strata they themselves and others have descended. When people elaborate on normative behavior or social customs, they tend to reflect the standards set by the nobility, or the ways commoners believe the nobility would behave or would handle various matters. This is typically reflected in statements such as: "Children are always free to play. They are never assigned any kind of work" and "Children are always given what they want. Their cravings are always fulfilled." I never heard a reference to the situation of slaves.

No descendants of royalty resided in Miang Tuu. Still there were large differences in the socioeconomic standing of the villagers. This is reflected in the upbringing of children from the time they are born and throughout their lives. The village is a socially dense community. Everybody knows each other; nobody can escape from the moral and other judgments of their fellow villagers. All residents know how all others behave and react in most circumstances. Their beliefs about others are confirmed in a vast number of encounters and observations.

To make too many generalizations about socializing processes in Miang Tuu, with its population of fewer than 200 individuals, would in many instances give a false impression. Although the ideological basis is related to a certain set of shared values, I shall try to overcome the problem of individual variations, or variations among households, by repeated comparisons between the household of *kepala lingkung* (the village headman) and various other households. *Kepala lingkung* is a noble; he and his wife are by far the most affluent villagers. His social position in the village is undisputed and unchallenged. This was clearly demonstrated some years ago when he refused to serve another term as *kepala lingkung*. During the period he was not in office, his social position remained unquestioned. In the village his household serves as a model of how others would have arranged their affairs if possible. The fact that *ibu* and *kepala lingkung* have their own dreams and share common goals that are different from those of other villagers is another matter.

Rather than showing a sharp horizontal stratification, Miang Tuu social structure is today a continuum with the *kepala lingkung* at one end. Most households are grouped toward the middle and the other end of this significant but rather short hypothetical line.

Babyhood and Weaning

When Miang Tuu babies are awake, they are constantly in the care of close relatives and are for long periods the focus of attention. Babies are often hugged and kissed by mothers, fathers, grandparents, and young caretakers. Fathers and grandfathers spend many hours with the youngest community members, especially before they are five years old. Men tend them when the mother is occupied but also when she is close and idle.

Mothers often bring their babies along when they work and when they walk to the market in *ibu kota* to spend most of the day there. Like all caretakers—men, women, young, and old—mothers carry babies and toddlers on their hips. From Miang Tuu it takes the mother about an hour to reach the marketplace. The daughters of *kepala lingkung* however, always make arrangements with other villagers to tend their babies if they have to leave the village. They are never absent too long and return home to nurse the baby there.

A crying baby is rarely heard. Miang Tuu villagers say that they all feel uncomfortable at the sound and will try to do something about it, no matter whose baby it is. If the mother is close, the baby will be nursed. If that does not calm the baby down, he or she is hugged, rocked in somebody's arms, and talked to (in baby language). Adults also often fiddle with the genitals of the baby to make it smile.

The only recurrent event that provokes distress to the baby and later the toddlers is the daily bath at the village well. Many young children cry every day for long periods when they are washed. The water is freezing cold, and when they get a little older and more mobile, water often causes pain because of the many scratches the youngsters have gotten during the day at play. It is interesting to note that although many caretakers may tend the young child during the day, only the mother and father will do the washing. In the memory of most children, neither the father nor the mother will be particularly connected to this pain-provoking act because they alternate the responsibility. The babies who are still not able to stand on their own are held closely to the body of the parent while water is poured over them both. When the child is able to stand alone, he or she is often washed before the father or mother wash themselves. But equally often the child can be seen clinging tightly to the legs of the parent, who pours the water over them both. Adults also usually regard the nightly bath as unpleasantly cold.

Another experience of early physical pain is of a quite different nature. Toddlers are often seen in despair when flies come and suck on wounds and open scars in their skin. It is impossible to escape from these flies and the pain they cause is quite severe.

Generally, Miang Tuu villagers agree that babies, toddlers, and the youngest children should have their way and never be punished for misbehavior. Because the child does not yet understand and is referred to as *bodoh* (stupid, not responsible for its actions), correction of behavior seems meaningless to the Miang Tuuans. This notion is shared by all the adult islanders. This might be important to later stages in the personality development of the population. The fact that fathers, when they are home, are much involved with the infant and share the basic cognitive interpretation of the baby's and young child's needs and emotional constitution makes the expectations of both parents similar. They seem to share values Erich Fromm describes as typical of matricentric mothers, as shown in their nurturant behavior during the first year of their children's lives (Fromm, 1970, pp. 103–105). In Miang Tuu, parents share the convention that nurturant behavior and love for the child should be complete during the first year. This behavior is not based on any expectation of rewards in the form of certain moral or social improvements in the baby's behavior. Neither is it expected that their love should be returned. Parents do not see any reason in forcing children to be what they cannot be or in punishing them for faults that are incomprehensible to them (the *bodoh* nature of children is a common notion in many parts of Indonesia; see, for example, Geertz, 1974, pp. 254–255).

Weaning is also gradual and not forced upon the baby. It is generally a gentle process. At the end of the second or the beginning of the third year, the mother may gradually begin to withhold her breast, unless the child is ill or miserable. If that is the case, the child is readily presented with the breast. Thus, one can often observe a child playing happily with age-mates when suddenly he catches a glimpse of his mother. Then the child stops abruptly and runs to the mother. If the breast is not immediately presented, the child will start to whimper until he has his will. The child then returns to continue playing.

People say there is no hurry with weaning. Children will gradually end suckling by themselves. Sickly children are purposely nursed into their fourth year.

After the first four or five months, the baby is handled in a relaxed and supportive manner that may seem gentle but also at times unemotional, almost apathetic. From this point on, mothers do not establish eye contact with their nursing babies regularly as they do with postnatal infants. Toddlers are nursed quickly, without overt emotional expression either from the mother or from the child. But if the child is sick or generally weak, the mother expresses empathy with him. A one-and-a-half-year-old boy was sick with malaria (*sakit panas dingin,* the diagnosis of the parents). After he had slept for twenty-four hours (neither the parents nor others who were awake at his side could wake him up) he regained consciousness. He seemed to suffer from cramps and refused to take any food. It was impossible to make him eat malaria tablets. His mother then ate all the malaria tablets in the house (approximately five) and nursed him as soon and as often as she had milk to offer. The boy accepted her breasts and his parents were convinced that the cure saved his life.

Women nurse their children at any time or any place while walking, talking, or working. Babies and toddlers are also fed during the night, often while the mother is half asleep. Mothers sleep close to their boys and girls until they are from three to five years. Mother and children keep company when the father is at sea. When the father is at home, the child may sleep between his parents or alone with the mother. The child does not have to be separated from the mother when the parents make love. Lovemaking is generally done when the parents believe their children are sleeping.

In most homes, all household members sleep on the floor; only in the more affluent homes is there more than one bed. It does, however, happen that toddlers and older children move to the bed of a grandmother in another house when their father returns from a long voyage. According to what people say, this is to prevent the child's being frightened if he wakes during the night and sees this stranger (the father) in the dark.

Attentive involvement between mother and suckling sometimes seems to be assymmetrical. Thus a child may be given the breast in such a way that it has to stand on its toes to reach up to it while her mother is sitting in a chair eagerly engaged in conversation, drinking lukewarm water, or nibbling on a broiled banana.

Other times mothers urge their child to nurse. One day, for instance, a young mother came out of her house on her way to the swidden. She looked around for her son. She discovered him playing with some friends. He was a healthy little boy between two and three years old. The mother called his name, once, twice. He ran to her. The woman squatted and made him suckle both her breasts. The boy acted impatient, looked like he hardly had the time, and soon returned to his playmates. The mother covered her breasts, picked up the *parang* (bush knife) and placed it on her head, and walked off.

Bonerate mothers are worried about upsetting their children by a too-abrupt or severe weaning and try to make the transition as gradual as possible. But a stricter procedure has to be followed if a woman becomes pregnant again too soon. She tries, however, even in that instance to make transition easy for the child. A mother who has a sister who is also nursing may be asked, or may volunteer, to share her milk between her own child and the nephew. (I never observed this.) A substitute wet nurse may also be hired, although this is possible only in the most wealthy households. Sometimes the weaner who wants to nurse is handed to a dry woman, and this may be repeated with gradually shorter intervals. Sooner or later, in most cases, the mother smears her nipples with pestled *lombok* (a variety of small capsicum pepper). A woman in her late twenties told with a smile that she still remembered the burning sensation in her mouth when her mother had applied *lombok* in that way.

If the newborn infant should die early, a recently weaned sibling would in many instances be nursed again, or if a wet nurse should be in demand the mother would take on that role.

The daughters of *kepala lingkung* nursed their babies for a shorter period than the average in the village. This is in accordance with the information their father gave: "Poor people nurse their babies for the longest period." This does not necessarily express any difference in the life expectancy for members of the different households, but the indication is clear. Only two of *ibu* and *kepala lingkung*'s seven children had died as babies or during early childhood. This is clearly below the average village infant/ young child mortality rate of 60 percent to 70 percent.

Miang Tuu weaning seems to create different early childhood experiences for the majority, who are gradually weaned between the age of two and three, than for the few who are weaned earlier in a more dramatically abrupt way. One should perhaps suspect that this would lead to a development of a high sibling envy by early weaners. That this is indeed so cannot, however, be easily observed in interaction. (I did not conduct in-depth interviews or apply any psychological methods that could have offered more information on this question).

Development of Motor Movement

Bonerate ideology is consistently rational on the point that the progress of motor development depends on the physical constitution of the child. Some children take their first steps before they are one year old, while others do not control motor movements at the age of three. The Miang Tuuans also agree that girls usually start to walk earlier than their brothers. Parents say children have their individual speed of development, and there is no reason to worry if a child does not toddle around at an early age. He will let go when ready. As already mentioned, babies are usually carried on the hip of their caretakers. According to some authors, this is an active way of transportation that strengthens the thigh muscles of the baby, unlike more passive means, like being carried on a cradleboard or in a shawl. Active transportation could contribute to an early motor development.

Miang Tuu babies are allowed to crawl both inside the house and outdoors. Babies are thus often, especially inside, seen crawling on their knees or, just as frequently, scooting along in a sitting position. This is very different from the Javanese way: "until the child's muscles are developed enough for him to actually support himself erect, he is not permitted to move about alone. A Javanese baby misses the crawling stage entirely" (Geertz, 1974, p. 256). Hildred Geertz seeks to relate this lack of an active, exploring stage of crawling and the habit of carrying babies on the hip to the widespread passive personality she finds in adult Javanese. Yet a similar passivity is present among Bonerate villagers. Here, at least, the developmental explanation must be different from Geertz's proposal.

Although walking is regarded as a natural accomplishment that will be mastered in time, Miang Tuu villagers do in reality stimulate at least some of their children to an early start. The unambiguous ideology related to this matter may possibly reduce a potential stress in the parents of late walkers; the child also avoids being ridiculed or teased for poor motor performance.

Babies are sometimes encouraged to stand alone and try to walk before they are a year old. Usually the father or another caretaker holds the baby in an upright position some 2 or 3 meters from the mother. She calls the baby and he is on his own. He might toddle toward the mother. If the distance is too long, the baby stops after having made two or three steps and bumps down onto the floor on his behind. This often makes him cry. If that is the case, the try is not repeated until some days later. Both adults and older children love to watch the baby's efforts. This is regarded as good entertainment, thus happy laughter and cheers accompany the first steps of many Miang Tuu children. Tini (granddaughter of *ibu lingkung*) made her first steps at an age of approximately eight months. At eleven months, she controlled her body movements well and was able to walk and run. She was rarely seen crawling. Before she was taught to stand and walk, she was an extremely fast crawler, but always in a sitting position, never on her knees.

In the house next to Tini's home lived a boy approximately three years old. He was not yet able to walk; when not being carried, he was sitting down or crawling about. He was small and had been sick most of his life.

Some parents of older toddlers make a walking device from a

bamboo pole that is split from the bottom and almost to the top. A crossbar is forced inbetween the two legs of the pole. The crossbar is for the toddler to hold on to when a caretaker takes the upper end of the bamboo. An old grandfather could be seen touring the village with his grandson holding on to the walking device. This happened daily for weeks while the toddler's mother worked on the swidden. The old man thought it was about time the two-year-old boy improved his walking.

The children of the *kepala lingkung* household had generally been early in walking. My information alone cannot explain why this is so, but some sociological determinants are interesting. If we look at the access to resources we find that, because in this household they were able to hire assistants to do various tasks both in the house and on the swiddens, they could put more effort than average into the training of their children. And just as important, this training could be done at the times when the mother, other family caretakers, and the baby were eager and energetic to play or practice. In most other households in the village parents are busy toiling long hours daily. When they return to the village both parents and child are tired. Also, single mothers whose husbands are at sea gain little by helping their children develop motor skills. It is easier to control a baby who does not move about too far or too fast. The same situation is experienced by the youngest child tenders. As long as the babies they are responsible for can be dropped and do not move far, the young child tenders are free to play. Toddlers need by far more attention than less mobile babies. I am not saying that these are the most important reasons that some children walk early and others do not in this community. There are children outside the *kepala lingkung* household who start off early. It is also likely that a child from that household could be late. Minor differences in diet and health surely also influence the speed of this development.

Control of Bowel and Bladder

Excretory training is not a dominant feature in Bonerate socialization. Babies and toddlers are gently urged to urinate before they are put to sleep at night. The baby sleeps close to his mother, wrapped in a tiny *sarong;* no precautions are taken to prevent soiling during the night.

After urinating or defecating, babies are washed with water. During the day babies and toddlers are usually undressed; diapers are never used. When dressed, babies are loosely wrapped in a *sarong;* they are never swaddled. Children never wear underwear. When child tenders carry a child they think will be urinating, they simply hold the child away from their body. If they are inside a house and if time allows, the child is carried outside.

During the two first years, the lack of bowel and bladder control is interpreted as another manifestation of the *bodoh* nature of young children and is thus treated matter of factly. No adult irritation can be observed; scolding never occurs.

The baby is not allowed to play with his feces, which are instantly carried away. The villagers say that cleanliness develops gradually, but at the age of two or two-and-a-half years, measures are taken to teach the child. If she is soiling inside the house, the child is carried out in a slightly rougher way than before. If she defecates on the village ground, adults who observe the act may smilingly comment on it loudly enough for everyone present to hear: *"massi bodoh"* (still stupid). The three-year-old is often brought along with his parents to defecate on the beach in the mornings. Defecation is not a private act in Miang Tuu. Although adults and adolescents cover themselves with their *sarongs,* the villagers sit closely together along the water line. They like this feeling of company on the beach. Husbands and wives usually go together, especially after sunset. (Feces in Miang Tuu always disappear by being eaten, swallowed, or washed away either by cocks, hens, dogs, or the ocean!) Although I did not hear the notion expressed, a child might come to feel that something or someone (an animal, the ocean, or other people) always wants his droppings. On the beach the dogs are often right there, trying to snap it away even before it cools. Adults do not like this experience, but they easily control the situation. To babies and young children the dogs are much larger, more disgusting, and may even be anxiety provoking, especially if the child is alone.

I could not find any indications that feces are considered an especially disgusting matter. To some degree the villagers are concerned about their own and their childrens' feces. They are examined regularly, especially when someone feels ill or a child is weak. The topics of conversation on this issue have diagnostic implications. People examine feces to determine the nature of their diarrhea and keep track of its duration, to check for the absence or presence of blood, and, especially in young children, to look for intestinal worms. (It is believed that if children younger than three to four years old eat fish meat, they are likely to get intestinal worms. These parasites are a health problem for many children in the village and often make their stomachs quite swollen.)

When a baby or a toddler soils himself, indoors or outside, he is cleaned instantly. The washing and cleaning is done either by the father, the mother, or whoever is in charge of the child at the moment.

A father was visiting a neighbor and carrying his baby boy on his hip. He seated himself on the floor and placed the baby on his lap. Suddenly the baby urinated and made the father soaking wet. The man stood up, asked for some water and washed his son. The remainder of the water was thrown on the bamboo floor to clean away the urine there. He dried his baby with a dry part of his *sarong,* left the child with a woman, and walked home. Not a single word of correction was uttered to the child. Soon after the father returned in a dry *sarong.*

A little girl is defecating while her five-year-old brother caretaker plays with some other children. He notices that his baby sister is sitting on her feces. While he collects some water and washes the girl with his left hand, one of the girls he has been playing with carries the feces away in an empty coconut shell.

Tini has defecated in a corner of *kepala lingkung's* house. Her grandfather finds the feces and tells his wife, who calls on her daughter, Tini's mother. She washes her baby while her two younger sisters dispose of the feces and clean the floor.

Tini is urinating on the floor while her grandfather is mending a fish net. He gets up and walks to the back of the house where he talks to his wife and Tini's mother. Soon he returns with some water, washes his grandchild, and cleans the floor. Finished, he picks up the baby girl, strokes her gently, and brings her to her mother.

I was not able to observe any differences in the instruction of bowel and bladder control among the different households in the village. Positive sanctions for early development of skill seem absent. Also there seems to be a high level of consistency between ideology and practice related to this issue.

Development of Speech

Miang Tuu villagers agree that the development of speech is also a natural accomplishment that will be mastered in due time. They say that girls often acquire some verbal skill earlier than most boys do. Because of an ethnically heterogeneous village composition, the language situation is somewhat complex (Broch, 1987). The major language mastered by all adults is the Bonerate language. However, other languages such as Bugis, Bajau, Selayar, and *bahasa Indonesia* (the Indonesian national language) are also in use. These are not merely dialects, as they are not mutually understandable. Most villagers are bilingual, some trilingual, and a few polylingual. In some households more than one language is spoken daily. The language of the marketplace is the Bonerate language. Civil and military authorities stationed in the *ibu kota* speak Bugis and *bahasa Indonesia;* the latter is also the language used for all instruction at the Bonerate schools (Broch, 1981, pp. 47–48).

When adults communicate verbally with infants and babies they apply a babbling baby "language": "They do not understand anyhow," parents explain. Compared to children of most Western societies, the development of verbal skills is a slow process in Miang Tuu. Few children start to construct sentences before the age of three; most at that age utter only single words such as *ina* (mother), *ama* (father), and partly mispronounced personal names. Neither the youngest child caretakers nor adult caretakers seem to talk much to babies and toddlers. However, they express their care by being close and by hugging and kissing the tiny ones. They are never left out of sight. When they feel uneasy, they are distracted from the source of stress by objects or by close body contact, not by verbal communication.

One of my neighbor's boys, who was according to his father three or perhaps four years old, had not uttered a single word yet. This boy was also physically undeveloped because he had long been ill. His older sister was approximately six years old; she too was seldom heard talking; even when she was playing with age-mates, although she had the ability.

A little baby girl learned to respond to the calling of her name when she was approximately seven months old. Her grandfather, who lived in the house next to her, heard her whimpering one night. From his place, well hidden behind two walls, he called her name and she responded instantly with a joyous shriek. This was regarded as great fun, so soon all household members in turn called on the tiny girl. She always replied in the same way. Her shrieks triggered lots of laughter. The show went on every night for many days.

This girl did not develop speech while I was in Miang Tuu, but there was little doubt that she was smart. Sometimes she imitated adult behavior in a way that attracted rapt attention from all present. When she was crawling in her sitting position along the floor, she stopped every time she saw a large gap between the floor boards. She cleared her throat and spat down to the ground below the house, just as adults do all the time!

Half a year later she carefully received all gifts she was given with her right hand (the clean hand). She had at that time also learned to use only that hand when eating.

What is reported among Fore babies also seems to describe those in Miang Tuu:

> An ever available possibility of exchanging meaning through touch was open to all Fore babies; even before they could talk, they were communicating needs, desires and feelings to a number of responsible caretakers by touch and physical movement. This constant "language" of contact readily facilitated satisfaction of the infants' needs and desires and made the harsher devices of rule and regimen unnecessary. (Sorenson, 1978, p. 17)

Tini is sitting on her grandfather's lap. Her female cousin, who is approximately five years old and who talks, is also present. The cousin starts to caress the man, and Tini, who wants his affection all to herself, gets jealous and tries to push the intruder away. When her effort does not help, she starts to cry. At the moment the five-year-old seems to yield to Tini's demand, their grandfather intervenes gently, telling the oldest girl to continue. He pats both of them on their heads and a little later they are both happily sitting side by side on his lap.

Responding actively to pervasive tactile and other nonverbal signals, Miang Tuu infants and toddlers soon recognize and accept as natural the affectionate responses they constantly receive.

A toddler who is just beginning to walk is having a hard time reaching her mother and is crying. But the mother is busy carrying one pail of water on her head and another in her hand. The tiny one continues to cry, but spots a five-year-old girl who has often been her caretaker. Now she totters toward her. The caretaker places the toddler on her hip and calms her down quickly. At this time the mother reappears; she has deposited the water and is ready to nurture her daughter who is now in a good mood.

Yobaida is approximately seven years old; she is a small girl. For some time she has been Tini's caretaker. One morning Tini is sitting outside her home close by her mother. From the other end of the village Yobaida is approaching, carrying her little brother on her hip. When Tini discovers this she gets sulky and starts to cry. Yobaida finds a compromise, she places her brother on her right hip and walks off giving Tini her left hand. All seem satisfied. But then apparently Yobaida thinks something is wrong. Now she tries to carry both toddlers at the same time, one on each hip. But they are too heavy and she is soon worn out. However, at that moment the little boy wants to do something on his own and Tini is alone with her caretaker.

Miang Tuu children develop verbal skills relatively late, probably because their social environment offers few incentives to encourage that development. The very complex language situation in the village where several languages are spoken also probably contributes to children's slow development of verbal skills. However, communication between adult and baby/toddler seems to be many sided and functional in the village context.

Attachment Behavior

Indicators of dependency (Rohner, 1975, p. 175) among Miang Tuu babies and toddlers are many. They cling to their caretakers, seek attention, and become jealous if they feel rejected because another person is favored. When they are separated from their mothers or waiting for or demanding nurturant response from someone else, they are unhappy, sulky, or tearful and often start to cry.

Miang Tuu babies are attached to their mothers, but also to other major caretakers—for instance, a grandparent, an elder sibling, or sometimes a young caretaker outside the immediate household. These attachment relations endure over a relatively long period of their life span (Ainsworth, 1977, p. 50). At Bonerate, intimate relations between mother and children of both sexes last through life (Broch, 1983). Informants also say that close friendships often develop between the young children who are child tenders and their charges. This is manifested by particularly close intimacy between two siblings or two children of different households. In the latter instance, however, this lasting attachment can be openly expressed only if both children are of the same sex or in some contexts in which they can claim to be "almost like siblings." Although Bowlby is particularly concerned with infant–mother attachment, he argues that there is no evidence to believe that young children diffuse their attachment over many figures and end up without strong attachment to anyone:

> When a child has more than one attachment-figure it might well be supposed that this attachment to his principal figure would be weak, and conversely, that when he has only one figure his attachment to that one would be specially intense. This, however, is not so: indeed, precisely the opposite is reported for both the Scots infants and the Ganda. (Bowlby, 1972, p. 367)

Bowlby concludes that

> There is a strong bias for attachment behavior to become directed mainly towards one particular person and for a child to become strongly possessive of that person. (p. 368)

Miang Tuu children both develop attachment with specific tenders and show attachment toward these bonds. It is important to stress this point because all young children and infants are likely to show attachment behavior toward any available figure (Ainsworth, 1977, p. 57). The major implication of the phenomenon holds true: a limited number of people possess the power to allay the infant's distress quickly. "Most children have a stable hierarchy of preference that is tied to the quality of the interaction rather than to its duration" (Kagan, 1977, p. 36). Miang Tuu child tenders are not playmates sought out by toddlers only when they are in good spirits. The child tenders are indeed sought for comfort and support when the toddlers are tired, sad, or alarmed.

In Miang Tuu the very availability of attachment figures and attachment-like figures through childhood seems to strengthen an anxiety about being left alone. Babies, toddlers, and other young children express fear of being left alone. At the moment a child tender moves away from the youngster she or he is taking care of, the child starts to cry. This happens even if other small playmates and their caretakers are close. If toddlers are playing together and one caretaker leaves, one of the toddlers will get upset, cry, and try to follow the one who left, even though the mother may be within reach. In an overwhelming majority of such cases the caretaker returns or some other person (mother, father, or substitute caretaker) lifts the toddler from the ground and hugs him for a while. Still worse is the experience of being left completely alone. The toddler has tantrums, screams as loudly as she can and beats the ground with her tiny fists. Villagers will run to comfort her. The caretaker, if it was a small boy or girl, will be verbally corrected by villagers present regardless of their kin relations to the toddler or the child caretaker. Ainsworth points out that both the frequency and the intensity of the activation of attachment behavior tells us less about the strength of the particular attachment bond than about the situation in which this behavior is activated (1977, 58). I never observed a baby in acute distress try to comfort himself by thumbsucking or any other behavior.

As a general rule Miang Tuu children do not play alone. When they do, they make certain, by calling the person's name at relatively short intervals, that an attachment figure is close by. Children do play in pairs, but most commonly they form play groups of from five to ten or more participants. Children at the approximate age of three-and-a-half and older usually do not cry when left alone for a moment. Instead they actively search out the company of others, children or adult. Children enjoy being close to adults and may in such instances play by themselves. Adults also express, both verbally and physically, at least a mild anxiety about being alone. Nobody likes to sleep alone in a house and one will always try to get company. The exceptions are some men who often fish alone from their dugouts and others who occasionally work without companions clearing a small swidden. Everybody agrees that it is best to have company. When men work alone, but are within shouting distance of others, they yell to each other at frequent but irregular intervals. When villagers go in groups of twos and threes to collect marine animals at night, they always call to each other from one group to the other so they know who is where. And they inform others when they return home. The same holds true when more than one man is fishing at night. To my knowledge women never work alone if they are outside the village. They arrange the work so they can keep in sight of one another and reluctantly move more than 40 to 60 meters away from the closest person. If they work at some distance from each other, they will walk to and return from the fields together. The distress at being alone that is present in childhood thus seems to continue into adulthood.

In the incident described in Chapter 1 (in the section called The Time of Pregnancy), Kartini was separated from one of her attachment figures. When her young aunt went on a voyage to Java, Kartini clearly suffered from the loss. She cried more than usual and would not let go of her mother. After some days Kartini, who was approximately ten months old, developed an attachment-like bonding to her new caretaker, Yobaida. To encourage the development of attachment relations, Yobaida slept with Kartini, and they also usually ate together. Little by little Kartini was again able to leave her mother for extended periods, now in the company of Yobaida. Typical behavior at this time was for Kartini to smilingly run back and forth between her mother and the little caretaker, both of whom would hug her each time she came close.

As the days wore on Yobaida played the role of an overwhelmingly nurturant attachment figure. When, however, Kartini's aunt returned from Java, Yobaida was totally ignored (she was in fact left in such an emotional and social vacuum that the observer felt sorry for her). Kartini clung to her tiny aunt and would not let her go, trailing her wherever she went all day long. When Yobaida called upon Kartini she did not respond at all. After a week's time it became obvious to Kartini that her favorite aunt no longer was as submissive to her moods as before and gradually she again turned to Yobaida for nurturant affection. When Kartini felt stress she searched for her mother or Yobaida—the one she first caught sight of or the one she thought to be closest. During most of this time Yobaida slept in the home of Kartini at night.

Most of the literature on attachment and attachment behavior agrees that the relationship between mother and infant leads to a particularly strong bonding and that this should not be correlated only to the fact that mothers nurse their children. Kagan argues that one possibility that explains why the mother appears to be more salient than substitute caretakers is that she is both more affective and more unpredictable with the young child and, hence,

is a greater source of uncertainty. Parents are more eager to interpret signs of mental and motor development in their children than
other caretakers, who are more relaxed about these matters.
Because the secondary caretaker is less personally involved, she is
easier to predict and does not become a source of uncertainty for
the child. The mother, on the other hand, appears to her child as
less predictable and harder to understand, but also a more frequent source of joy and excitement.

> The typical mother is emotionally involved with her infant, and more
> likely to display strong affection and to convey emotional charged
> messages. In addition, she holds the standards by which she judges the
> child's development, and she watches for deviations from them. One
> may believe that any defiance of her authority is a sign of future rebel-
> liousness, and she quickly reacts to it with disapproval or punishment.
> (Kagan, 1977, p. 37)

Surely Miang Tuu mothers are major attachment figures, but I
would claim that the young child caretakers also serve this function to a degree that makes it difficult to regard them solely as substitute attachment figures. It also seems reasonable that Bonerate
attachment development is partly based on a different foundation
than the one Kagan is proposing. This variation may give us the
opportunity to show that different patterns of socialization may
serve the same ends. This also means that Kagan does not present
a universal model with cross-cultural validity. A major difference
appears in the Bonerate islander's notion that young children and
babies are *bodoh*. Neither parents nor other caretakers have particular developmental goals for the baby or toddler. Even at a later
stage, Miang Tuu parents are not particularly ambitious for their
sons and daughters. The overall attention during the first years is
focused on the survival of the baby. As described earlier, a consequence of this is that the infant must be named properly and must
be able to thrive and be happy. Love in this context is not regarded
as reciprocal. Love and affection is given to the baby without any
expectation of immediate returns. Given this ideology, the differences between the mother figure and other caretakers are reduced,
and their behavior is more uniform than in the general case presented by Kagan. In Miang Tuu the youngest caretakers even have
their own food resources. They collect and prepare delicacies such
as tiny clams, snails, and sea urchins that they share with the tod-

dlers. In this way they have, as do the parents, access to positive rewards in the form of tasty food that they can give to the babies they look after. All the same, in Miang Tuu mothers remain the primary attachment figures.

Kagan does not consider the qualities of young caretakers, although he is much concerned about the effect of ordinal position within the family (pp. 50–54). Given an institutionalized system of young child tenders as in Miang Tuu, the dilemma experienced by firstborns may be somewhat reduced compared to that in many Western societies. This is because the quality of the relationship between child tender and baby is not affected by later born siblings. The system grants a high level of emotional continuity between baby and tender. The young child tender offers the toddler an adequate model better adjusted to the toddler's mental and physical developmental stage than the omnipotent mother (and father). We might then assume that the young child tender in some instances also serves to delay or lessen the tensions related to the transition from babyhood to childhood. The child tender is more available as an attachment figure than the mother can be when a younger sibling is born. This does not say that the two attachment figures share the same qualities or can fulfill the same needs for the toddler. Neither does this undermine the social importance of the mother figure as a primary focus of Bonerate attachment. Given the Bonerate culture's matrifocal elements with uxorilocality (see Broch 1983), it is perhaps not strange that fifteen-year-old girls and newly married women say that they would never leave Bonerate for an extended period of time because they would miss their mothers too much. But young men also said they preferred to live at a place from which they now and then could visit their mother.[1]

I did not observe significant differences in the attachment behavior of the children of the various households in the village. Some differences could, however, be observed in who the chosen attachment figures were. *Kepala lingkung*'s daughters were among the few who had child tenders recruited from an outside household on a permanent basis. The household composition at a given

---

[1] During my stay in Miang Tuu, I was at first puzzled by the recurring interest both men and women showed in *my* mother. Did I not find it hard to be so far away from her? They pitied her for my staying on Bonerate; she surely had to be out of her mind with grief. They never asked about my father or wife. When I wanted to talk about them, the Miang Tuuans returned to the subject of my mother.

time is important in this connection. In newly established households or those with few members, the father (if and when at home)
is more engaged with child care than in households that include
more members. In these latter cases the mothers spend fewer hours
in direct association with the baby. Boys are also more often
engaged as primary child tenders if no sisters are close to them in
age. And, finally, in households where a young girl is hired as a
permanent child tender to a baby of another family, her brother (if
present) will be looking after their own youngest sibling (if there is
one). I shall return to the role solutions and the behavior of these
young child tenders when examining the second phase of Miang
Tuu child development in Chapter 3.

Aggressive Behavior in Babies and Toddlers

Miang Tuu children are born into a society that is
protective and gentle towards its youngest members. From the
onset of life this behavior is regarded a necessary prerequisite to
the survival of the baby. This does not mean that Bonerate men
and women never become exhausted from waking at night when
babies are crying or sick. Actually, they hate the sound of crying,
which is only accepted in its institutionalized form at the time of
death. Thus, prolonged crying is also regarded as a sign that death
is nearby or has already entered the village. People will do almost
anything to prevent or stop a baby from crying. If this result is difficult to achieve, the villagers do not direct their anger or irritation
toward the baby, but rather they seek the cause of the problem. A
baby cries because his needs are not fulfilled by his caretakers.
When crying gets on one's nerves, actions of displaced aggression
may be observed. For instance, a cat may be kicked for no obvious
reason other than that it is close. The usual way to handle these
matters is, however, to summon a caretaker and to say in a matter-
of-fact tone that the baby is crying.

After we had all been awake for long hours because Tini cried
almost continuously during the night, my tired host told me, "If it
were not for the fact that Tini is still being nursed, I would have
had her in this house. When her mother [his daughter] is tired, she
does not care. She lets Tini cry, she does not take her up, she does
not nurse her, she does nothing! I have to get up, walk across to
her house, pick up the baby, and calm her!" He did do that some-

times, but just as often he summoned some other household member to do it. His expression may reveal displaced aggression toward the baby, but also surely primary aggression toward his daughter who did not "master her mother role" as he would have liked. One important thing to notice is that his speech showed very little emotional involvement. He talked about the episode first thing in the morning, but in a completely normal, matter-of-fact way. It would not make sense to be angry with babies or young children who do not know how to behave. Also to show aggression toward his daughter or to nag her would be shameful. All adults are supposed to control their emotions.

Bonerate child-handling practices provide a setting where the baby is exposed to little aggresssion. Notions common in our Western societies, such as "getting even" of "putting one down," or our subtle ways of withdrawing affection or mocking are never directed toward the youngest household members in Miang Tuu. As with the Tahitians, "They feel they must take adequate care of the child—not to do so is a matter of severe community shaming—but this care is not considered particularly difficult" (Levy, 1978, p. 226). Occasionally there is gossip about Miang Tuu parents who others claim do not fulfill the needs of their babies.[2]

Experimental and accidental aggressive acts, as well as object- or goal-oriented aggressiveness, are sometimes carried out by babies and toddlers. A girl who wanted to suckle her mother's breast got angry when there apparently was no milk for her. She squeezed the breast with her hands, and those standing close by laughed. The mother tried to direct her daughter's attention to a pet chicken.[3] The episode shows how Miang Tuuans typically deal with baby aggression, which is considered a natural consequence of the child's nature of being *bodoh*. The baby did not

---

[2] Here, however, unlike the Tahitians, people are indeed reluctant to bring gossip or criticism directly to the criticized. That is regarded as impossible, even dangerous, because if the matter is grave the offended may be so shamed that he will have to react. To criticize somebody for a serious thing is like placing a person in a corner without possibility of escape!

[3] Adults sometimes try to stop overt aggressiveness by means of laughter. During one year in Miang Tuu I witnessed open display of hostile aggression three times. At two of these instances, both of which were related to the same conflict, there was verbal combat with threats of physical violence. During the combat the villagers gathered and shouted at the combatants, made stupid remarks at them, laughed at them, and finally made almost all the dogs in the village bark. In both instances it became impossible to carry on the quarrel;

understand the impact of an aggressive act. Adults regard this as funny. No attempts are made to punish the baby, and the target of the aggression does not show anger or irritation. The typical reaction of the "audience" is to regard such incidents as entertaining.

Some of these features can be demonstrated further in a rather unusual example. The setting is the typically relaxed village scene where adults and young community members sit together in the shadow of the coconut palms. Men and women chat, watching some of their children who are playing. A little boy who has just learned to walk is happily toddling about. A little girl, somewhat older than the boy, pushes him from behind and he falls. He turns around with a surprised look at her. She laughs and hits him. Her approximately ten-year-old caretaker picks up the "naughty" girl. The boy's father puts his son on his feet and brushes off the dust from his naked body. The father then walks to the girl, now sitting safely on the hip of her caretaker. The man gently slaps her hand until she starts to cry. This obviously alarms the tiny boy, as he starts to cry. Before that moment he seemed merely bewildered. His father lifts him up and carries his crying son to the weeping girl. He takes the boy's right hand in his own and slaps the girl, who screams loudly. Her caretaker walks off with her, but the father, who has been smiling all the time, runs purposely clumsily after them. At this play, all present, children and adults start to laugh and suddenly the two crying children break out in laughter.

The episode is atypical in several ways. It is extremely rare to see expressions of physical aggression, even among children in the village. Perhaps that fact offers an explanatory clue to the improvisation of the father.[4] The girl caretaker reacted in the prescribed way when she interrupted the fight before any damage had been done. She did not correct the naughty girl, nor did she withdraw her affection from her. But the father broke generally applied rules

---

however, the cause of the conflict remained unsolved. If *kepala lingkung* had been in the village—he was on Java at the time—there would have been no quarrel, the villagers believed. He would have solved the problem and made the combatants behave. I asked him about that when he returned. He had great confidence in himself in that matter and said the villagers were right, he would have stopped the quarrel. "People should not behave like children." He viewed their loss of emotional control as regression to children's behavior.

[4] He has the reputation of being an exceptionally strong man (on one occasion he beat up a man from the neighboring village on the beach because that man had been unfair to a Miang Tuu wife) and of being a hard-working, good-tempered, kind, and at times funny man.

of conduct, one after the other. He returned aggressiveness from a child and he slapped the child of another villager, not once but several times. He made his own boy return an assault with more aggression. I do not think all villagers could have acted successfully in that way. Forcing borders, he made use of his undisputed good reputation and managed to turn the event into a show. He never acted as if he were angry or irritated. At the end of the performance he emphasized that this indeed had been a show by his "toddler-like" way of running, and he made everyone laugh! If he really had been irritated by the aggressive little girl, he demonstrated (by quite a skillful performance) his ability to keep his emotions under firm control!

Miang Tuu babies and toddlers who are well of course show emotion in various contexts—at times, as we have seen, with aggressive tendencies.[5] Sometimes they get angry and may pout or sulk if their demands for food, goodies, and attention are not met immediately. Children younger than five are rarely away from the supervision of their caretakers and an adult, but not necessarily a parent, will always be close.

In spite of the unusual case presented above, the Miang Tuu setting resembles that of the Kalahari !Kung:

> Not only are aggressive models scarce, but the adult technique of interfering at the earliest stages of discord means that the child usually doesn't have the opportunity to learn the satisfaction of striking and humiliating another child. This situation, of course, is made possible by the fact that children and adults occupy the same close living space and by the fact that on any typical day there will be many adults in the camp (or in the village on Bonerate) who are keeping an informal watch on the children. (Draper, 1978, p. 37)

When the toddler manages to go down the house ladder to the ground without assistance, he is heading "in the direction of childhood"; when he is talking, he is in the middle of that transition. This implies that the child now is capable of some verbal instruction, and, most importantly, the child can be given his first assignments. The child is still far from ready to control his emotions; however, children are from now on encouraged to try to conform. A seven- or eight-year-old child is no longer unambiguously *bodoh*

---

[5] Some young children in Miang Tuu appeared apathetic, but their flat affect seemed to be related to poor physical health and illness.

when angry, but rather *gila*, which is closer to our understanding of *stupid* and *crazy*. In this period of transition, there is a gradual diminution of indulgence by the parents, which is reflected at a somewhat delayed speed in the behavior of other caretakers. The child is pushed away from the center of household attention. The child has by now survived the most critical years when child mortality is at its highest. The child experiencing the parents' withdrawal of patience and indulgence usually reacts by entering a period of strong display of passive aggression in unfocused rage, temper tantrums, and sulking and often begins to appear sullen and depressed. This phase lasts for an indefinite period. Even after the child has seemingly recovered, he can suddenly return to this behavior upon encountering social difficulties he cannot manage. For example, a baby sibling is given the only remaining piece of candy, which the older brother wants. At such times both ten- and thirteen-year-old children occasionally regress to temper tantrums, although it gradually happens less frequently. I shall return to this phenomenon and other forms of aggressive behavior when discussing Miang Tuu childhood in Chapter 3.

In some contexts the youngest children are taught to fear strangers. This is sometimes related to specific circumstances that exist at the time children are becoming more mobile. The impact of this informal teaching is greatest when the child has acquired some verbal skills. Then she listens to adults who recall frightening encounters with strangers and superhumans. Besides the fact that young listeners cannot easily be barred from adult discussions, the villagers want their children to fear outsiders. My impression is that Miang Tuuans find themselves living in a world that in many different ways is a hostile environment. The basis for this attitude is in part historically acquired and perhaps not always a currently valid interpretation of the situation. Childhood memories of many villagers, however, offer dramatic and very strong reasons for not trusting outsiders. Many men remember how frightened they were during the early 1960s when the *Gerombolas* were pirating the waters. At that time the villagers always kept a watchman on the beach to report as soon as a *perahu* was spotted on the horizon. Every time that occurred, all males who were between thirteen and forty years old fled the village to the hinterlands. There they stayed hidden, sometimes for several days and nights, until the danger was over. If men remained in the village, the *Gerombolas* forced them to join their *perahus* as crew members. If a villager refused, he was killed on the spot. According to the villagers, *Gerombolas* never hurt women. Before the *Gerombolas,* during the Second World War, Japanese soldiers came across the sea, and before them the Dutch. Today there are strangers to worry about, including Bugis police and military personnel who are present on the island.[6] During my first months on Bonerate I never met women or children when I walked about alone. I often saw them far away working on the swiddens, but when I came close they were always gone, hiding somewhere.

Similar fear of strangers is reported from several other Southeast Asian communities. On Java children are taught to fear strangers (Geertz, 1974, p. 259) and the same is true among the Semai (Dentan, 1978).

But to the Miang Tuuan strangers are not the only potential danger. In the sea man-eaters such as sharks, barracudas, moray eels, and stingrays, all believed to be dangerous, are often encountered. In addition, there is a host of various fish and echinoderms with poisonous spikes, some of which are thought to be able to kill an adult and many able to kill a child. Even if they are not killed, children and adults can be in great pain for extended periods after touching some of these animals.

Bonerate islanders also firmly believe in giant octopuses and know where they are most likely to be confronted. At night these octopuses may engulf even a large *perahu* with all its crew!

Spirits or ghosts also live in the sea. As far as I know, they usually do not harm humans, but it is regarded as unpleasant to hunt for fish at the location where these spirits are abundant. One can hear them talk and feel their presence but never see them, the villagers say.[7]

Many of the villagers also fear thunder, which bites and kills, but not lightning, which never harms people. Some people have seen the tooth marks of the thunder where it had bitten trees. Thunder is especially dangerous if one is alone at sea.

---

[6] When I left the island for a short break, I was seriously warned to stay away from all strangers and never to ask a Bugis *juragan* to take me back to Bonerate unless he said he knew *kepala lingkung* well.

[7] The spirits prefer places with large table corals under which they live. They had one favorite location quite close to Miang Tuu. It was also said large bad sharks often appear there, and strange things have happened at the same place.

The only time I heard about an instance of physical punishment of children in Miang Tuu (I never saw such an act), was when *kepala lingkung* told me he just had beaten some four- to five-year-old boys. They had paddled the open sea in a dugout canoe. The boys were not skilled swimmers. "They have to be afraid, so that they never do that again. I have told their parents that if this happens once again, we shall find a way to punish them also (the parents)."

Children often have difficulties in distinguishing fact from fiction and in realistically assessing potential danger (Bowlby, 1972, vol 2, pp. 230–231). The stories told in Miang Tuu are narrated as facts of life, which, from an emic point of view, they are. This makes it difficult for the child to distinguish among the various objects of fear. When their curiosity is great, children overcome some fear by banding together. Thus, when I walked in the narrow streets of Baranka/Bonerate, the twin *linkungs* comprising the island *ibu kota,* bands of small children usually trailed me, shouting and screaming at me with joyous terror. The fright was reinforced by some adults. Some times a man would grab a small child and call out: *"Belanda* [white man], would you like this one? Take him with you. He will be a good worker." The child would start to cry and cling desperately to the adult, not daring to look at me. This never happened in Miang Tuu. Before my arrival in the village, *kepala lingkung* had gathered all the parents and ordered them to tell their children and make them understand that the *belanda* should be left alone. When I arrived, all children, toddlers, and babies were let into the house, which soon became completely crowded. Here they were allowed to watch me for approximately two hours. After that they did not show signs of being frightened by the sight of me. However, a toddler from a different village who visited Miang Tuu with his mother became extremely frightened the first time he saw me. He screamed and clung to his mother while the Miang Tuu children had a good time laughing at his reaction.

Some weeks before I arrived in Miang Tuu, a Bugis civil servant was stoned by Miang Tuu children when he was about to enter the village alone.[8] Nobody stopped the children because nobody saw or heard it. That day there were only children home in the village,

---

[8] Interethnic relations in Miang Tuu are described and analyzed in Broch, 1987.

people said. It should also be noted that some authors (Burton & Whiting, 1963) have pointed to a high level of correlation between the absence of fathers and mistrust of strangers and the development of aggression.

Although aggression and even occasions of overt hostility are described and discussed here, these incidents are not a normal part of everyday village life. One can live for several months in Miang Tuu without any such incidents. It is a quiet community where life passes at a moderate speed without many highlights. Life is a monotonous effort to make a living. The Miang Tuuans are indeed gentle in their interactions within their village. "Relatives do not fight, and in this village we are all related like one big family," one of my informants said. However, I believe that given appropriate circumstances much aggression is projected toward objects outside the community.

Rituals of Safe Passage

Rituals of safe passage are designed to protect or maintain a sense of identity during periods when undesired changes may occur.[9] Like most rites of passage, they are generally structured into three-stage sequences: an initial stage, a liminal stage, and a stage marking the final outcome of the ritual. The liminal stage is initiated by rituals of separation and concluded with rituals of aggregation. Whereas rites of passage are designed to alter the status of the initiates, rites of safe passage ensure the status of the initiates. Three different rituals of safe passage are commonly conducted in Miang Tuu: bedtime ritual, sickbed ritual, and ritual of safe voyage. Here we shall pay most attention to the first two of these rituals, those with which the young children are most directly involved.

Babies are fed, carried around, and put to bed at night when they fall asleep by themselves or when the mother goes to bed. Toddlers are usually put to bed around seven thirty or eight o'clock, just after supper. Children of approximately four years and older stay up as long as they like, but are sometimes asked if

[9] The idea of rituals of safe passage originated in an article in the *Journal of Psychological Anthropology* by Stuart Albert, Terry Amgott, Mildred Krakow, and Howard Marcus, "Children's Bedtime Rituals as a Prototype Rite of Safe Passage" (1979, pp. 87–105). This discussion is thoroughly influenced by that work.

they are not tired. This clearly indicates that their parents think it is about time they retired. But if the youngster says no, that settles the case. Disputes about bedtime never occur; however, the whole village goes to sleep between nine and ten o'clock most nights and children never stay up alone! When the full moon is up, children sometimes roam about outside longer than usual.

Before the child goes to sleep, she changes clothes. That is, she puts on a *sarong* for the night. She might get help or do it herself, depending on what her age is and how tired she is. Sometimes she also asks her mother to help her in order to attract her attention. A parent rolls out the sleeping mat for the child. She then lies down while the mother seats herself beside the child and strokes her hair while she hunts for lice. Most nights it is the mother who does this, and often she continues to stroke the child well after she has fallen asleep.

Brothers and sisters may share the same sleeping mat lying close together. Also a young caretaker may sleep close to the child she is in charge of during most of the day. Sometimes women work late during the night—for example, picking corn from the husks in preparation for a feast. In such instances the sleeping mats of the children are rolled out on the floor next to the busy mothers.

Miang Tuu children occasionally wake up crying from nightmares. The parents will be right there to comfort the child by stroking him, sometimes lighting an oil lamp and singing lullabies.

In the middle of the night, *kepala lingkung* and *ibu* are talking together; they walk across to the house of their daughter. I can hear them talk for about thirty minutes before they return. It was the ten-year-old Owati who woke up from a terrible nightmare and scared her two older sisters of fifteen and twenty-two. Kartini, the baby of the house, did not wake up.

During a corn-party, *kepala lingkung*'s five-year-old son fell asleep. When we were ready to leave, the boy was still sleeping. Nobody wanted to wake him up, so he remained in the house, where he was quite comfortable—it was the house of his maternal uncle. In the middle of the night we heard him yelp, and soon he was carried to his own house in the arms of his uncle. When the boy had awakened, he wanted to be brought home.

Children are usually lazy in the morning and are late risers. They stay quiet and must usually hear noises from the fireplace before they are ready to sneak some food. They are often some-what irritable; their parents excuse them as not being yet awake. They go outside to urinate or may go with their parents to the beach. After they are fully awake and the sun is up, they are usu-ally washed.

If we interpret the sleeping procedure as a ritual, the initial stage is when the necessary preparations are made. The sleeping mat is rolled out to mark the proper setting. The child is undressed, a new *sarong* is put on, and the child lies down, but he is of course still awake. The ritual of separation consists of the "presentation of gifts." The mother presents her child with "gifts of her presence, affection, and nurture." She convinces the child of her concern and his lovableness. She convinces herself and the child that everything will remain all right through the night.

When the child wakes up the next morning he will be the same person, still entitled to the mother's love and affection. If the child thinks his mother is finished too soon with her demonstration of nurture, he may protest, thus signaling that he wants additional evidence of her caring for his needs. Almost every night the mother will stay close until her child is asleep.

The liminal stage of the ritual is the sleep itself. During sleep, the child is separated not only from his parents, but from all friends and caretakers. However, many things may happen during sleep. Strange dreams and even nightmares may be confronted. Bonerate people pay heed to some of their dreams, so in that sense their altered state of dream consciousness is an important part of their lives. Still, the sleeping individual is as dead, yet he is living and even experiencing things. The state of unconsciousness may in some contexts be dangerous. The sleeping child needs protection. Protection is granted by the significant others who are present if the child should wake up.

> Since the sleeping person cannot hear or see those around him, those around him may carry on conversations as if the person were not present. The person who is asleep, is for many purposes, treated as invisible. His ties with others have been temporarily severed. (Albert et al., 1979, p. 88)

When the child wakes up at an unscheduled time—for instance, because of a nightmare or in some strange setting—he reacts by being afraid and sometimes by not knowing where he is.

> During the night a child may run to his parents for comforting. In fact,
> it is the child's potential access to his parents during the liminal period
> of his rite of passage that provides him with a needed sense of security.
> (Albert et al., 1979, p. 89)

After the nightmare, the parents reassure the child of their presence and care and his own safety by repeating the love-affirming
separation rite to make the child sleep once again. Because the
darkness of the night in itself is frightening and conceals the familiar waking world from the child's perception, they bring light so
that he can see they are his parents. The fact that the mother is the
preferred one to put the child to sleep and that it is her name I
heard called at night may indicate that she is the first-priority
attachment figure of her children. The husbands, who always
assist their wives during the nights when they are home, probably
do so not only to comfort the child but also to encourage their
wives. Bedtime rituals are never conducted when children want to
sleep during the day.

When the child wakes up in the morning, she reassures herself
of the whereabouts of the other household members. She makes
her presence known and when her parents think she is too quiet,
they ask her if she does not feel well. In that way she steals the
attention of other household members and makes them show concern about her well-being. The household members are reunited
by this ritual of morning aggregation. The child reenters society
with the same rather than with an altered identity.

> In summary, sleep is a time when identity change is threatened, and
> just because there are similarities between bedtime and those occasions
> that promote a change of identity (the individual is separated from
> society, is in a weak and vulnerable position, etc.) special rituals are
> needed to ensure that his identity is maintained, and ideally strength-
> ened. (Albert et al., 1979, pp. 88–89)

If we remember the high child mortality rate in Miang Tuu, it
becomes even more plausible that both the child and her parents
find comfort in the bedtime ritual.

Another example is the liminal state of the sick child. Parents
work to prevent the sick child from reentering unconsciousness,
which is thought to be most dangerous in that context.

When children suffer from what is considered a minor illness,
their parents are especially alert during the night to assure the

child that they are present. They also want to assure him and themselves that everything will be all right. Grandparents and siblings will often take turns to let the parents catch some sleep. The normal procedure when a child is ill is to strengthen the common bedtime ritual. But if the child is thought to have a fever, the Miang Tuuans get worried and want to keep the child awake. "If a really sick person sleeps during the night, he may sleep forever," one informant explained.

Kartini woke up in the middle of the night; she was crying and wet with fever. Her mother picked her up and carried her while she sang to comfort the tiny girl. After an hour or so, Tini's maternal grandparents went across and took turns singing and walking the sick child. At sunrise all three adults were dead tired. Tini's fever had dropped, they said, so it would be appropriate for her to sleep now. All day someone was close by and whenever Tini started to cry, she was picked up and sung to. By the evening, she was thought to be well enough to be put to sleep. She slept normally through the night.

During the nights in Miang Tuu, one could always tell if there were sick children in the village and could identify their homes by the songs sung to them (the villagers rarely sang in other contexts). If a seriously sick child should fall asleep, villagers would gather to keep guard; the patient must never be left alone.

Tjatjo has been lying down with a high fever for several days. We can hear him shout and babble through the walls. A little later his mother starts to cry. That signals that she is afraid her son soon will die and that it is time the villagers pay the home a visit. Nobody has any idea about the nature of the disease. Tjatjo is an only child. His three siblings all died in early childhood before Tjatjo was born. A continuous flow of villagers, mostly women, pays their visits, many of them nursing their infants at the sickbed. Outside the house, village life goes on as usual.

After dinner *ibu* and *kepala lingkung* walk across. It is dark and an oil lamp is lit and placed below the house. Tjatjo's mother does not cry any longer. The fever has dropped a little. The sick boy, wrapped in two or three *sarongs,* lies on the floor on a sleeping mat. His mother sits close by, as do the father, an old man, and two women. Tjatjo moans; he is unconscious. The wakers touch him all the time and pay attention to the beat of his pulse. They are interested in the condition of his feet, in whether they are moist or dry, and they want to make sure he is warm. To sweat is always a good sign, then your body is working, the villagers say. The father bends toward the head of his son and says gently, "You must wake up." The old man (a ritual expert, dismissed two days later and replaced by another expert) asks the others to raise Tjatjo to a sitting position. Two women are steadying the limp body. The old man pinches the boy's ankle. Tjatjo moans so low that he can hardly be heard, keeps his eyes shut, and draws his breath heavily a couple of times, then coughs gruesomely. The old man pulls Tjatjo's hair, but there is no visible reaction. "You must wake up," his father urges him. The old man kneels behind Tjatjo's back and murmurs a spell; we cannot hear the words. He blows at the neck and the back of the boy before he is laid down again. A few times Tjatjo opens his eyes, but he does not fix his sight. "You must wake up," his father repeats. But Tjatjo does not move. Visitors come and go; every now and then the wakers touch the body of the sick boy. They place his arms on his stomach and lift them down again. The women are most active. People watch over him all through the night. The midwife who delivered Tjatjo and another woman who was present at his birth have come to the house. The father does what has to be done in the house, such as gathering water and boiling it. He buys tobacco for the wakers who take their turns and sit chatting and smoking continuously night and day. Neighbors prepare food for *ibu* and *bapak* Tjatjo. (Just before I left Bonerate Tjatjo was on his feet again, but not completely recovered).

If we now look at the sickbed procedures in terms of a ritual of safe passage, we first observe that all the attention is directed toward the liminal stage. Somewhere during what should have been an everyday ritual something went wrong. The precautions made to provide a safe passage were not strong enough, because other forces were at play and the child became seriously sick. What is now important is to wake the sick child up and take other, stronger measures to prevent a threatening change in both his status and personality. When the unconscious person regains consciousness, it is overwhelmingly important to keep him awake until he is believed strong enough to sleep. Then and only then, the nurturant gifts will provide the child with the necessary confidence to regain his previous status after the sleep.

Tjatjo was not a small child—his age was approximately sixteen years—but I do not think age matters in this context. That forces struggle over life and death during the liminal stage was clearly shown by the reactions of the villagers when Tjatjo, two days after the night described above, seemed to regain consciousness for a while and then passed out again. For that period the boy was in a terrible rage. He shouted and cried, scolded his mother, and demanded to be moved away from her house. He refused to eat and ignored his father. Although possession was never mentioned, the villagers agreed that this was not really Tjatjo. One of my friends, however, admitted that individuals never behaved like ordinary people after a disease like this one. But then they never lived very long.

Tjatjo's parents were shaken with fright and stunned. *Bapak* Tjatjo left the house red-eyed from many nights awake. He turned to me and repeated several times in a murmuring voice: "He does not know what he is doing to his mother. This is not Tjatjo. You know this is not Tjatjo?" From the house we heard Tjatjo's continuing rage. (It is interesting that when the boy finally recovered somewhat, he stuck to his wish to move. But he gave a more acceptable explanation for his wish: he needed a softer place to lie down! He was really skinny at that time and not able to walk.)

During the liminal stage your "spirit" may travel far. The ritual activity is directed to bring the true "self" back to the human body.

The event that finally signals to all villagers that life is back to normal (or as normal as can be) is that the reconciled individual thoroughly washes himself or is washed by his parents at one of the village wells. Thus, after having been considered mystifying and perhaps frightening, the child is again regarded as clean and safe. In other words, normal patterns of interaction are again possible after the ritual of aggregation is concluded.

The third ritual of safe passage is quite explicit in its most relevant symbols. The context is that of Bonerate *perahu* sailing. Fathers and other men leave the island for as long as eight months, during which time there is no communication with the relatives left behind. The open sea is regarded as dangerous; it sometimes happens that a sailor or even a whole *perahu* never returns. Before the *perahu* leaves the island the sailors are accompanied on board their ship by close relatives. They sit chatting together for a while and the crew serves a tiny meal, a symbol of lasting relations and mutual trust. The sailors give away food as a demonstration of their nurturant affection toward the family members they now leave behind. The family members show their concern by their presence. Usually the *perahu* is anchored quite some distance from Miang Tuu so they all have to walk for an hour to say good-bye. After the meal the guests are paddled ashore and the *perahu* is ready to start her voyage. Good-byes are, at least on the surface, a completely unemotional, matter-of-fact performance. The children are playing and joyous. To shed tears at this time would be a mistake, showing one's doubt about the undertaking or anticipation of no return or of death.[10] During the liminal period the sailors are invisible to those staying home and vice versa. If the *perahu* remains absent much longer than anticipated, the villagers have magical means to get information about how the ship and crew are doing (Broch, 1985a). At the return all crew members hand out gifts, presented through their wives to their children. Thus they demonstrate their acknowledgment of the status quo. Everything remains the same; they have not altered their interpretation of their own position vis-à-vis wives and children. Stressing ritual aggregation in this context may be particularly important, given the fright of the youngest children in the village at the sight of all these "strangers." One of them may even claim to be your father and steal (some of) your mother's attention!

Other Aspects of Daily Interaction

Although the socialization of the youngest children is mild and gentle, some restrictions limit their activities. Before they gain motor control there are few problems, but when they start to move about, certain areas are regarded as dangerous. Thus toddlers should never be left alone. Likewise, children who are not yet able to swim well are not allowed to paddle a dugout canoe in deep water. Children usually learn to swim around the age of five. Because the beach cannot be seen from the village, young children are not allowed to bathe except in the company of older caretakers. This seldom creates any problems because there are almost always adults on the beach. Another activity that is

[10] By contrast, three days before I finally left Bonerate, one of *kepala lingkung*'s married daughters told me she would cry when I left. And at the time of departure both the married daughters of the household cried, thus telling everyone that they believed in no return or reunion.

regarded as dangerous to children younger than approximately six years is collecting coconuts. Children of this age are not allowed to climb the palms. When *kepala lingkung* one day saw a four-year-old boy at the top of a palm, he ordered him down at once. Later he summoned all the villagers and told them that if parents did not manage to keep an eye on what their children did, the parents would be punished. Two other times during my stay *kepala lingkung* threatened all parents collectively in this way. One incident has already been mentioned—when kids had paddled a canoe on the open sea. The other event that brought this reaction was when small boys were playing with rubber-string fish harpoons in the village. *Kepala lingkung* would never specify to me how he would punish the parents; instead he would say, "We shall find a way and they all know it!"

This does not mean that children are kept away from everything that might hurt them. A generally practiced deference to the desires of toddlers and older children in the choice of play objects permitted them frequently to handle sharp knives, large *parangs,* sharp pieces of scrap iron, and fire. Their acquaintance with such items makes most four-year-old girls and boys fully capable of opening green coconuts with a *parang.* I believe that a dichotomy between culture and environment as perceived by the villagers is reflected at this early stage of child socialization. The surrounding environment is to be feared, whereas the community and all common tools are to be trusted. LeVine suggests that the ways parents rear their children

> are rational in that they contain information about environmental contingencies previously experienced by the population and assimilated into its cultural tradition . . . [and in] that this information concerns not only features of the environment that are most salient to the health and welfare of the child but also appropriate responses to them. (LeVine, 1977, pp. 53–54)

It is not the dugout canoe that is dangerous, but the ocean; it is not the coconut that is dangerous, but the intrusion of the environment into the village by tall palms, which may hide scorpions and centipedes. (Palms may even kill people during storms when they are uprooted and fall through the roof.) However, tools used incorrectly are banned, as in the case of improper handling of harpoons.

Before the age of four to five years, boys and girls are treated alike in most contexts. They do the same things, and they are given the same toys, such as scraps of paper, empty boxes, coconut shells, and an occasional top made from a mangrove tree seed capsule. Babies and toddlers, boys and girls are also frequently given pet animals, usually tiny chickens. A string is attached to its foot and the toddler drags it behind him or sometimes carries it under his arm, just like the big boys carry their fighter cocks and hens. The chickens are brought into the house and fed; they are, however, not shown affection. The child is not taught to care for it or to feed it. The chicken usually dies after a few days, sometimes only to be replaced by a new one.

Although baby girls and boys are generally treated in the same way and both run naked most of the time, their gender is emphasized. All girls have their ears pierced at about the time they are named. Most of them wear tiny earrings. Some boys wear amulets around their necks, usually a coin. Other baby boys wear an *agar akar* (black alga) bracelet around the wrist, as do many sailors, to protect them from drowning. The first haircut of boys is also celebrated with a Koranic reading and a meal.

Mothers often decorate their baby daughters with colorful flower bands. The youngest boys and girls like to pick flowers, but that interest is soon gone, only to reappear in the mothers of female babies and in adolescent girls, usually when they tend the babies of others.

As already shown, some minor differences in the childrearing pattern are related to the social position of the children's parents. Other differences may have some relevance to the development of sex identity in the children. Only the most affluent households can afford sex-symbolizing clothes for their youngest members. Thus their toddler boy may be dressed in a garment resembling an army general's uniform and his tiny sister may have far more dresses than her playmates have. In this way, their sex is emphasized and their social position is contrasted to other children of the same age within the village.

When the child is able to run about and has acquired language control, his world is widening. He is entering childhood.

Tini is held by her aunt, Owati. Infants often exhibit attachment behavior to more than one individual.

Fathers spend many hours with their toddlers.

Although baby girls and boys are generally treated in the same way, their gender is emphasized. All girls have their ears pierced at about the same time they are named and most wear tiny earrings.

One feature of a family's relatively high social position is sex-symbolizing clothing for children.

Although they are not directly involved in much daily religious activity, children enjoy watching the adults pray at the village mosque.

Miang Tuu children like to help their parents in the daily chores.

The mother-daughter dyad is strong and lasting.

Children enjoy playing in the shaded area under the village houses.

All Bonerate boys and girls are circumcised and the associated rituals are an important village event. Here a novice sits in bed at the beginning of the ritual.

The novice is brought home after the ritual is completed.

After their puberty rites girls take on more tasks. Here a girl is peeling cassava.

Adolescents are very concerned about their appearance and like to dress in their finest clothing.

CHAPTER 3

Miang Tuu Childhood

When children have gained motor control, their world gradually widens. They are no longer guarded by child tenders wherever they go, and their trips away from the home become longer. Within the village few restrictions set limits to their activities. All homes are open and the family members welcome visitors. However, the child is typically *malu* when visiting the homes of others and feels completely at ease only in his own household. In the homes of their playmates, children are quiet onlookers. Usually they stand close to the entrance, watching what the hosts do. They are alert to anything that is said or anything that happens. What they may have noticed before now becomes explicit. For example, there are great variations in the living conditions of the villagers. The houses range from one-room huts made from palm leaves to two-room gabled houses with partly wooden floors and walls, front verandah, and attached but separate open-fire kitchen. A few families own a bed, whereas most villagers sleep on the floor. Some villagers have a table and a few have two tables; some have chairs, while others have no furniture. The children also learn that the food available to family members differs in both quality and quantity from one household to another. Thus they soon experience that many villagers are different from themselves, and that these differences cannot solely be related to occupation alone. Adult villagers generally do the same things—they work on the swiddens, fish, gather coconuts, or work as sailors (Broch, 1985b). Some people own more coconut palms, clear larger swiddens, and accumulate more material goods than most of the villagers. In addition, some parents work for the parents of the child's friends, but that work is not reciprocal. Children of some households run to the more affluent neighbor to beg for a piece of fish, meat, or other food, but if you are poor nobody comes to your home on the same errand.

Children of all villagers, both boys and girls, play together in various contexts. But sometimes play groups are formed of members of the same sex. Generally this division is more frequent among the older children. However, small boys are more often observed playing with older girls than are small girls with older boys. Groups of young children thus explore the environment surrounding the village. The older are in the lead, the younger trailing behind but never left alone. The youngest are allowed the time they need to keep up with the others. All children of the village are seldom together at the same time. The play groups split up and rearrange themselves, although some children tend to be best friends and stick together most of the day. Groups of children drift along the shore. Sometimes they may dig for bivalves or marine sandworms, and other times they just play in the water. If adults are working at gathering sea urchins during low tide, the children often join in the activity. Or if men are fishing, the children may sit down to watch them. At other times, small bands of youngsters roam about inland, visiting adults working on the swiddens.

Most of their time is, however, spent in the village. Here they can often be seen sitting down in the shade rather passively for as long as thirty to thirty-five minutes without much talking or other expressive behavior. Children seem to be content to sit around adults when the latter are working. The children may sit quietly, just watching, for an hour or so. When they get a little older they may be asked to help, but quite infrequently. How often they are asked depends on the type of work and the mood of the worker.

During my stay in Miang Tuu I never observed a child inflict pain on a playmate by hitting or another openly aggressive act. When children cry, it is not because other children have teased them or been physically rough. Crying is most often provoked by anger toward parents because of the child's inability to cope with conflicting wishes and cultural standards. This is especially common when a child demands attention that is offered and given to somebody else. Children also often cry when their wishes for various material goods, such as a particular food or a play object, are denied or simply ignored. Children sometimes make their playmates cry by refusing to share a valued object. Crying children are not comforted but are generally ignored. They may occasionally be scolded for being too angry or crying too much. This often sends the crying child into strong temper tantrums. I do not think it is a coincidence that in Miang Tuu the children of the most affluent households generally reacted more strongly when denied attention or material objects than their somewhat poorer friends did. Common experience and both popular and learned ideas about how children are spoiled would tend to corroborate this difference in behavior of children of unequal socioeconomic status. However, when I suggest that children of the richer villagers tend to be spoiled, that is only compared to the other children *in the same village*. I do not want to develop a universal explanation of how children are spoiled but only to evaluate significant differences in behavior within a Miang Tuu-defined cultural frame.

Bonerate childhood generally provides freedom and room for leisure, but children experience minor frustrations caused by the necessary adjustment to decreased attention from others. Sometimes the child may find it hard to understand why her parents no longer are available for comfort to the same degree as before. One day a girl sat with five women, one of them her mother. They were burning garbage, and the smoke hurt the eyes of the girl. She stretched out her arms toward her mother, but neither she nor the other women moved to help or comfort the girl. Neither did they tell her to move away from the smoke.

Children are supposed gradually to understand the nature of many things and to begin to control basic elements of their behavior. Although this takes a long time to learn and adults recognize that regression to babylike behavior is natural for the child, they remain firm.

Because they have not developed a mature mind of their own, children are generally not punished. However, they will begin to understand through experience that they no longer are the focus of all attention. Although parents restrain their emotions during interaction with their children, they always keep an eye on them when possible. Parents like to know where the children are and what they are doing. When the parents are not in the village, they always make sure that other adults are watching, although this vigilance seldom interferes with the doings of the children.

The parental lack of emotion in many encounters with children is in no way complete. In several contexts parents, especially mothers, demonstrate affective love for their children. It could, however, be said that the adult now shows affection when it pleases him and not necessarily at the same time that the child demands contact. Bedtime rituals performed every night, goodies handed out, and a thorough examination of the hair to kill lice are typical expressions of parental care. As we shall see, self-centered children gradually adopt some of these ways to express their own feelings in interaction with playmates and the babies they are tending.

To adults, village life is often monotonous; to children, this is less so. Their activities are more diverse. Children are not burdened by too many chores and are given the best of many aspects of life. They sleep when they want to, cook their own small meals, and often receive the best pieces of food and fruits gathered for the household. During the season, children gather lots of sweet mangoes that they may or may not share with their parents. Generally children are reluctant to share their goodies with adults but are more generous with their playmates. However, the youngest children sometimes find it hard to share their best food with anybody and often eat it hidden from the sight of all others. Children are seldom urged to share.

Birth, sickness, intercourse, and death among both humans and animals are all part of daily village life. Children are not barred from these events. However, I never observed evidence of children copying such life crisis incidents during play. Sex play between boys and girls seems absent. Adults have indeed told the children that they would not tolerate anything like that. When, however, small boys and girls touch and play with their genitals, this is ignored and not commented on.

The strong aversions related to incest are also related to the supernatural punishment the villagers believe results from incestuous relations:

> It happened in the old days that young boys and girls [in their late teens] fell in love and committed incest because they did not know how they were related. That is why parents usually arrange the marriage of their children to make sure every bit of information is known about all kin relations. When incest occurred, the offenders were placed together in a large bamboo *bubu* [a kind of fish weir] and sunk in the sea. If that was not done, some major disaster would occur, such as a heavy storm and thunder that could ruin the village, or rain would

not fall during the wet season. Thus incest is not a matter between the two, but the act may destroy the whole community.

Miang Tuu girls should remain virgins to the time of their first marriage. But when I asked about the consequences if a bride proved not to be a virgin, the villagers responded with little understanding. To raise the question was close to an insult. Nobody remembered a relevant case!

Mating animals are usually ignored, although adults sometimes shout to an unwilling goose that she should not run away like that! Once when the gander caught her and bit her, a young Miang Tuu mother told the bird off: "There you really got it." Children do not seem to pay much attention to the copulation of animals, but they enjoy watching the "violent" behavior of the gander. Mating horses attract the attention of young and old, both of whom like to sit down to watch the large animals. Often they will comment on the act in a rather matter-of-fact way. This reaction is very different from the enormous excitement all villagers express during the yearly horse fights that take place between their houses. The arranged fights are attended by all children and adults; even visitors from all over Bonerate come to share the excitement. The village roars with shouts and laughter (this ritual is examined in the section Children and Animals in this chapter and in Broch, 1985a, pp. 278–279).

Children obviously witness their parents having intercourse during the night. The adults do, however, try to be discreet in their lovemaking. They restrict the act to the time when they think all the other members of the household are asleep. Sometimes children stay overnight in the house of a friend or a grandparent. That is a common arrangement when a husband and father returns from sea.

Children also listen to adults when they talk about sex. The contexts of these conversations differ, but some situations are rather typical. Young men often boast about their escapades in faraway harbors. When the wives listen to these stories they often react with openly expressed disapproval (Broch, 1983, p. 155). The stories do, however, probably add to the romantic imagination the children share about the sailor's life.

In Miang Tuu people gossip about unfaithful women who live in the *ibu kota* and supposedly have sexual relations with other men when their husbands are away. Miang Tuu women also tease each other sometimes by saying that it would be good to have a partner other than their husband for a change. But such remarks are never made in public when their husbands are present. When women talk together, they do not avoid such entertaining themes because of listening children.

Young couples occasionally argue because they feel their partner has been showing off in front of other villagers of the opposite sex. A woman or a man may have been particularly gay or sung in an affectionate way, for instance, in the presence of others. Such incidents are rapidly interpreted as sexual courting. Only unmarried youths should behave like that. I mention this because it all adds up to the lore of adult life that the children are likely to create in their minds.

Incidents of severe sickness or even death in the village do not influence or disrupt the daily life of most children. They are brought to the sickbed to pay respect or simply accompany their parents. The children are also curious to see the sick. But outside again, their play and mood are not affected in any noticeable way.

When a Miang Tuu woman is heard wailing hysterically, everybody knows that someone has died or is dying. To a European, it is at first somewhat puzzling that all sympathy and empathy is directed to the grieving woman (the mother or wife) and to a lesser degree to other close relatives, but not to the sick or dead. Both adults and older children react similarly, showing verbal concern for the "poor mother" or "poor wife" of the sick or deceased person. These two status positions are singled out and emphasized in most instances. Crying in this context is culturally required, so nobody tries to calm or to stop a crying mother. The intense crying lasts for a day or two, interrupted only by calling the name of the diseased and questioning why this had to happen. During the nights that follow, female relatives and older children from the village keep the grieving woman company. The same is done to comfort a man if his wife dies. Female villagers stay with him during the first nights after the loss.

Burial ceremonies are quick and involve only the closest kin. Death affects other villagers to the extent that they avoid activities that bring them in close contact with the sea. Thus fishing is prohibited and children are not allowed to swim or play in the water. These restrictions are, however, eased just a few hours after the burial is completed. The burial site is close to the village. Although children never play there, they are not afraid to go there. The graves are not tended. Usually the villagers do not mention or even speak about their dead; their affection and care is for the living.

Children are not directly involved in much daily religious activity. Like pregnant and nursing women, they are not supposed to fast during Ramadan, the sacred month of daily fasting prescribed by the Koran. Sometimes children tiptoe outside the windows of the village mosque to watch the adults pray. In some homes the children observe both their mother and father at daily prayers, but this experience is by no means common to all youngsters growing up in the village. In other households all members gather regularly for *pakande* offerings.[1] Many Miang Tuu villagers do not find the *pakande* custom in accord with their faith in Islam. Thus religious display is another cultural expression that creates differences among the villagers. In the households where the adults do not consider *pakande* offerings proper, the men condemn the custom more severely than do their wives. Their children are not allowed to bring offerings or to accompany others to the altars. In this way children soon learn that what others may do might be forbidden to them.

The Return of Sailors

I have already pointed out some potentially traumatic experiences of young children at the homecoming of their fathers. Young children sometimes find it difficult to understand why these long-absent strangers steal so much of their mother's attention. But returns from long journeys are also times of great expectation and happiness to the children who are old enough to remember their fathers. Every day, when the villagers believe that one of the *perahus* carrying Miang Tuu crew members is due to return, they keep watching the ocean from the beach. They try to identify every passing *perahu*.

When the sailors enter the village, children are excited and swarm around them. One of the first things the crew does is to visit *kepala lingkung*'s house, where they are served tea. The sail-

---

[1] A *pakande* is literally a small meal, here presented at small bamboo altars to thank or to ask for supernatural help.

ors are asked about the voyage, the route they sailed, wind conditions, health of the crew, and other Bonerate *perahus* they have met. The room is crowded with children who listen. The children of the *kepala lingkung* household are privileged and may sit close to the crew. The rest of them keep some distance; many stand by the door while others settle on the verandah.

Wives greet their returning husbands without much overt affection; they simply say it is good that everything is well.

During the first day the crew is home, their children and wives gather in the home of the *juragan*. This is the moment they have all been looking forward to. The *juragan* always brings lots of goodies, such as candies, toffees, and sweet biscuits, from Java. The sweets are all given to the wife of the *juragan* and she distributes them, making sure both children and adults get their share. It is an asset to have a husband and father who sails with a generous *juragan,* because most sailors return rather empty-handed from the journey. A good *juragan* "fathers" his crew or *anak anak kapal* (children of the ship). His wife keeps track of her distributions, holding back goodies for the absent. She makes sure this is a day of joy to *all* Miang Tuu children by handing out sweets also to those whose fathers did not join the voyage.

The children peel off paper wrappings and stuff themselves, eating two and even three biscuits at a time. They cannot be eaten too fast! No other day matches the homecoming day of a *perahu* from Java.

The day is also a great event for adults, but they may sometimes find it difficult to understand their babies' wishes. In a mother's attempt to do the best for her child, she tries to force a candy on him. The tiny boy, seeing a candy for the first time in his life, spits it out. His mother looks surprised at him. She picks the candy up from the floor and puts it back into his mouth. He takes time to taste it this time, but spits it out again. This is repeated several times before the mother gives in. By now the boy is sticky from sugar. He wants to nurse and has no interest in candy. The mother shakes her head, sucks the candy herself, and offers the boy her breast.

After all goodies were eaten one little boy remarked; "When I some day return from Surabaya, I shall bring even more *gula gula* [candy]."

Assignment of the First Chores

When children are from five to six years old they are delegated their first chores of importance in the daily activities of the household. They are by now regarded as old enough to be significant contributors, able to assist in a variety of different tasks. The assignments are, however, always adjusted to their physical age and mental maturity, as interpreted by their parents. The children are still not regarded as capable of heavy work such as most agricultural labor, netfishing, and other activities that require physical strength. The assignments are, however, regarded as important to the household. Bonerate children are not, as so often happens in Western societies, asked to do things just to keep occupied in order not to disturb tired adults.

Two tasks that are among the first to be assigned are highly repetitive—bringing water home from the wells and being a caretaker of a younger child. These are daily duties of many young Miang Tuu children. The only duty that clearly restricts the child's movements is to be a child tender. All other tasks are of short duration, and in most instances the child is free to stop working at a task as soon as he is tired or bored.

Most Miang Tuu children, boys and girls, have during one period of their childhood been a major child tender with the responsibility of looking after a younger child several hours every day for months.

Young boys and girls are given equal workloads and asked to do the same things. When they are about ten to twelve years old, a gender role differentiation gradually develops. The differences that are established are, however, few and not absolute. For some years the boys have already been eager to perform such tasks as gathering coconuts from the palms, fishing, or cutting brush when new swiddens are prepared. From this age they may be asked to assist in these activities. Few girls take part in such occupations, yet most activities are not strictly gender related; a boy is not ridiculed for helping his sister, neither is a girl teased for helping her brother. When the girls grow older they also begin to participate in heavy agricultural work and some few become very skillful fishers (these are of Bajau origin, see Broch, 1981, pp. 7–8; 1987).

Some children do, however, have to work more than others,

depending on the composition or the economic and social status of their household. The consequence of such differences is that until puberty children of the more affluent villagers have more leisure than their playmates. At the end of this chapter, I shall compare the duties of two boys and two girls from different households that reflect this socioeconomic variation in the village.

Generally the oldest members of a sibling group will have more duties than the last born. The obvious reason is that the same workload has to be distributed among fewer household members and newly married men usually spend most of their first years as husbands at sea. Also, a boy who is the firstborn child will be more involved, and for a longer time, in child-care tasks and other slightly feminine chores than if he had an older sister. The important issue at this point is that although a vague sex differentiation with regard to tasks develops from the approximate age of ten, no boy or girl is ridiculed by adults or by other children because of the kinds of tasks he or she performs.

Child and Sibling Caretaking

When children are given responsibilities in caretaking, they frequently have to adapt to two simultaneous sets of pressures, those from their small charges and others from their parents and other adult villagers. Adults always try to keep an eye on how the children are doing.

> Child caretakers must learn to balance these two sets of demands; they must try to understand often complex social rules; and they must correctly interpret the behaviors of the children for whom they are responsible. (Weisner & Gallimore, 1977, p. 172)

Usually interaction between caretaker and charge runs smoothly. The organization of different play activities is influenced by the extent to which caretaking duties are a part of the Miang Tuu children's daily life. Occasionally the duty is experienced as too heavy and in conflict with other interests and wishes. This is especially likely to happen when a child tender wants to play with age-mates who are for the time being free from caretaker duties.

Moane had placed "his baby" on the ground close by where he was throwing "marbles" with some friends (using *kemiri* nuts or candlenuts). Suddenly the baby started to cry. Obviously irritated, Moane made faces at her. He threw another marble, but when his sister continued to cry, he returned the marbles to the girl he had borrowed them from. Angrily, he picked up the baby and placed her on his hip and walked around to calm her down. By the time his tiny sister was comforted, some other children had borrowed the marbles and Moane was not let into the game again.

What is reported from Samoa also holds true on Bonerate:

> This fear of the disagreeable consequences resulting from a child's crying, is so firmly fixed in the minds of the older children that long after there is any need for it they succumb to some little tyrant's threat of making a scene. (Mead, 1968, pp. 32–33)

The caretaker knows too well that there is no excuse for allowing his charge to cry. The first adult who observes the scene will scold him publicly; in this way caretakers are soon taught the responsibilities of their task. But Miang Tuu children are no angels, and sometimes when they believe they are unseen they purposely tease their charges. Whereas Samoan child tenders are more indulgent than their parents toward young children (Mead, 1968; Weisner & Gallimore, 1977, p. 172), Miang Tuu caretakers are less predictable than parents in their interaction with babies and toddlers. On Bonerate, as in many other places, it also seems to make a difference to the caretaker if he has to look after his own sibling or a child from a different household. The youngest children receive somewhat rougher treatment from their own siblings than from other caretakers. One day I observed two children, a boy and a girl, who were looking after their younger siblings. They moved to the edge of the village where the toddlers were teased until they started to cry, to the great amusement of the caretakers. They continued to trouble their charges for a while before they picked them up. Then they returned, hugging the crying youngsters and showing all villagers how kindly they tried to comfort them!

At other times the caretakers clearly enjoy the duty; they laugh and play together with the toddlers. The caretaker may provide toys, she may catch a butterfly and tie it to a sewing thread for the charge to hold on to, or she may decorate the youngster with flowers.

Other good times are when adults, caretakers, and charges are all together. The adults find amusement in the play activities of their children. The caretakers are busy coordinating duty and fun. But in this setting they are not let out of the play if they have to turn away for a moment to comfort a baby. As soon as a baby or toddler whimpers, the adults remind the caretaker of his or her duty. But the problem is easily overcome. The caretaker can claim that the baby is hungry and wants to be nursed. The atmosphere is generally relaxed. When tired or in need of attention, the care-taker curls up by his or her own mother who will search for lice in the hair of her child, while the baby or toddler rests in the arms of the caretaker or plays close by in the sand.

Child caretaking is among the most responsible jobs children are assigned in many cultures. There are, however, striking differences in the types of caretaking mothers are willing to delegate, the age at which they consider a child trustworthy, and the amount of supervision regarded as necessary (Whiting & Whiting, 1975, p. 95). In Miang Tuu both girls and boys are entrusted with the care of younger children. This is important because this type of work seems related to the development of nurturance and responsibility. These personality traits are used in many societies to describe a feminine character. Where girls are delegated the responsibility of child care and other domestic chores, but their brothers are free to play, assist their fathers, or receive training in what is regarded within that culture as a male occupation, any difference in male/ female personality should become confirmed or strengthened by such an early task division. As we have seen, both Miang Tuu girls and boys develop skills in guessing the needs and motivations of their small charges. They learn what behavior is required to satisfy these needs. The caretakers are also made to understand that certain areas of the close village environment could be dangerous to their charges and thus have to be avoided. They are not supposed to bring them to the beach unless they are in the company of adults. They must never take the charges into the water. They must make sure the baby or toddler does not come close when coconuts are harvested from the palms. The consequences of their failure to adhere to these cultural prescriptions are clear: igno-rance or negligence can lead to injury or death of the baby or tod-dler. The tasks of caretakers mirror closely the Barry, Bacon and Child definition of nurturance (Rohner, 1975, pp. 179–180).

Helping Mom and Dad

Separating work from play is often problematic. The children's conceptualizations often differ from those of their parents. Whereas children are prone to regard as work all activities they carry out to help their parents, the latter often stress the irresponsible character of most children's activities and call it play. So also at Bonerate. The child sees himself as working as long as he wants. The adults, however, identify the same activity as play because, as they see it, the child pays less attention to the outcome of the activity than to his own boredom. The child is entertaining himself, not providing for a family or a household. To make believe denotes play activity, whereas "the real thing" is work. On this issue the Miang Tuuans, young and old, readily agree. Thus adults may excuse themselves for a poor performance by claiming that it was play. It is harder for the child who wants recognition to gain support for his view that it is the activity and not the situation that defines work!

Miang Tuu children are eager to help their parents in various ways. Both girls and boys beg their father for permission to come along on fishing expeditions. Children also wish to participate in agricultural work and the gathering activities on the beach. One day permission is granted, but the next day a similar request is refused. At home the father can tell his children not to come along to the field or the fishing locations, but when the children show up some hours later, instead of being scolded they are usually allowed to participate! Children's help is often a burden that prevents the adults from doing effective work. Both men and women recognize this, but because the children have to learn the Miang Tuu ways of livelihood, they are permitted to make mistakes. When they make work more difficult for their parents, the children are not blamed for the poor outcome. In this context the notion that children are *bodoh* applies. Children who do not yet understand the consequences of their actions should not be punished or scolded. Fathers sometimes encourage sibling rivalry and envy among brothers and sisters. For instance, an older sister may be denied participation in fishing while her younger brother is permitted to join. In this way, the father is explicit about his gender role expectations, but he is not consistent. Some days he brings his daughter along, but as she becomes older, he is more and more reluctant to do so.

The position of mothers differs from that of their husbands. Many of their daily routines are better fit for children's participation than their husbands' activities are. A mother often stays in the village, and much of her work is physically lighter than the more typical male work. But, most important, her need for help from the children is greater. When a husband is home he is part of the household team, but the wife is often alone for long periods and has to administer all domestic tasks on her own. Therefore, mothers are less prone to refuse help from their children than the fathers are. Mothers usually do not consider sex roles relevant when they delegate tasks or accept assistance from their children. The physical age, abilities, and wishes of the children count most; all tasks have to be done anyhow. The children observe that when their father is home their mother restricts her work in some areas she tends when alone. When the father is home, he does the heaviest work; when he is gone, the mother manages anyhow. If a task is particularly heavy, she may get help from a male villager. When a father returns from sea, his children observe that their mother directs much of his work in the household.

Children assist their parents in various ways. Many different goods are bartered in Miang Tuu. Most of these items are natural products, such as fish, turtle eggs, fruits, and mildly fermented cassava *(tape);* and sometimes they trade cookies made from corn, grated coconut, and other locally grown products. This trade is in the hands of the village women. Mothers engage their sons and daughters between the age of seven and twelve years to barter the goods. The children learn the price of their commodity, but when in doubt they run home for advice. Adult villagers never sell such items but the sale is a favorite work for most children of this age. Boys and girls carry what they have to sell on small trays placed on their heads. While they walk around the village, they cry out the name of the product and its price. Those who want to buy call on the young traders. The wife in a household that lacks children of the right age summons her neighbor's son or daughter to do the selling. The child is given a small payment in kind for the job. If a father has made a large fish catch, the husband, wife, and child may walk off to *ibu kota,* where the child sells the fish in the streets. The first time they do this, children usually find the experience frightening because there are so many strangers in the "large" island capital. But soon such trips are regarded as highlights of the year.

Girls tend to barter more goods than their brothers. This reflects the position of Miang Tuu women as household treasurers (Broch, 1983, p. 151).

During the seasonal peaks of agricultural labor, at times of sowing, harvesting, and the clearing of new swiddens, Miang Tuu appears a very quiet village. The children like to play and work close to where their parents work; they are allowed to help in most minor tasks. But children are seldom patient enough to stay with what they are doing for more than thirty minutes or so. Children are not urged to continue once they show signs of boredom and tiredness. Adults say that labor in the fields is too strenuous for children because it is physically rather hard work, and also the strong heat from the sun exhausts children quickly. On the swidden land shade is scarce and water has to be brought from the village.

Older boys are allowed to join a communal work group *(gotong royong)* when, for instance, large areas of brush land are to be cleared.[2] To the boys, it is great to be able to join in because they will be together with many men, some of them perhaps from other Bonerate villages. Participating in the task group gives the boys a feeling of age and gender recognition. One day during *gotong royong* a twelve-year-old boy was cut badly in his foot by a sharp *parang*. The boy working next to him accidentally injured him. Neither of the two boys was blamed for the accident. In the eyes of the villagers, they were excused because this was an accident and everyone knows that children do not concentrate on their tasks but play while they work. The men who had been working nearby were criticized because they had failed to prevent the accident. They should have directed the boys to work further away from one another. Such accidents are rare.

I have mentioned that children often reduce the output of their parents' fishing activities. When the children are excited and eager to help, they soon forget that they have to be careful and watch their movements to avoid frightening the fish away. However,

---

[2] *Gotong royong* is a widespread institution in Indonesia that appears in many different forms (see, for instance, Koentjaraningrat, 1961).

when the villagers apply *pandita* (a plant poison), the cooperation of children is welcome. During low tide, the *pandita* is thrown into the lagoon, where the poison dilutes and paralyzes the fish, which then sink to the bottom. Children and adults wade into the shallow water and pick up the motionless fish. Because most of the fish are small, not longer than approximately five centimeters, it is difficult to find them all. This is a work the children enjoy and are eager to participate in. They are, however, never allowed to mix or touch the *pandita,* as it is regarded as lethal even in small quantities if eaten by humans.

Family Structure, the Absent Father, and Cross-Sex Identity

Two features of Miang Tuu family structure and household composition can be singled out as crucial to an understanding of Bonerate socialization—periodically absent fathers and matrifocality. Not only is residence matrilocal, but the Miang Tuu society is also clearly matrifocal. Mothers are the focus of emotional, economic, productive, and reproductive attention (Broch, 1988). During the first years, mothers are principal caretakers and delegators of their children's tasks. The fact that most men and fathers, for several years, spend extended periods at sea reinforces the dominant role of mothers vis-à-vis other household members. Put a little differently, it could be said of Miang Tuu women that they both mother and father their children. It would thus not be surprising that the socialization of children in such a mother- and woman-dominated environment has a manifest impact on their personality development.

> The values involved are not specific to situations of infants and child care, but are seen as derived from broad orientations associated with the social system and its institutional goals. The function attributed to such values in child rearing is that of preparing the individual, through processes not yet well understood, for participation in that system, at some psychic cost to himself. (LeVine, 1977b, pp. 15–16)

Household structure, ecologic adaption, religion, and economy —as parts of the social organization—directly influence the socialization of children. The household structure is perhaps the most important of these factors. The focus here is not on kinship structure, but rather on the basic dyads found in every kinship setting. There are eight basic dyads in all societies (husband–wife, father–son, mother–son, mother–daughter, father–daughter, sister–sister, brother–brother, brother–sister), but all dyads are not given the same emphasis in different kinship systems. Thus when one kinship system gives emphasis to one or more of these dyads, the others are reduced in importance and modified in their content. What is important in the present context is the kinship content determined by the focus placed on the dominant dyads of social interaction (Hsu, 1972). Obviously the household structure reflects the cultural emphasis the members of a society place on basic kin-based dyads. In Miang Tuu, two dyads are stressed above the others: that of mother–daughter and mother–son. Of these lasting dyads, the mother–daughter relation is the strongest, both through time and in the mind of the villagers. Two other dyads are also stressed by Bonerate culture, the sister–sister and husband–wife dyads, but neither of these is as firm and emotionally fixed as the two mother–child dyads. The Miang Tuu dyads that are emphasized here have one thing in common. They are all formed by a female link that in two instances is the mother. This picture would be even more striking if we renamed the husband–wife dyad as the husband–wife/mother dyad. This renaming is based on the hypothesis that Miang Tuu wives often serve as mother substitutes for their husbands (Broch, 1983, pp. 155–156).

Repetitions are always part of socialization processes. This makes arguments related to many such processes somewhat circular—for instance, when we examine how dyads are maintained as major kinship foci within a culture. Based on cross-cultural findings, it has been claimed that there is a high level of correlation between a household organization that allows alternative caretakers of children in addition to the social mother and an emotionally warm and nurturant socialization of children. It is regarded as highly significant that the mother is not tied to the household sphere because of never-ending child-care duties. In societies where mothers are not able to get away from their nurturant role even for brief moments, additional births are often met with ambivalent attitudes and mothers often develop aggressive reactions toward infants and young children. The upbringing of children in such societies is felt to be burdensome to the mother, who is in total charge of the young and is therefore restricted both in her movements and social interaction (Whiting, 1980; Rohner, 1975).

In Miang Tuu not only do women gain social prestige when they become mothers, but the society also is arranged in such a way that the young mother is not isolated with her child. She can, after a period of rest, continue to perform the tasks she did before giving birth. In Miang Tuu, a new mother is not forced away from important economic activities or other productive tasks because of her new social role. As we have seen, alternative caretakers are always at hand to assist the mother. This fact may in part explain how the emotionally important mother–child dyads last through the life span of individuals and why they are repeated through generations. Within flexible limits, the Miang Tuu mother leaves her young child when she wants to, knowing he is well cared for. Later she returns when she feels like it. Miang Tuu parents do not experience the problems of many city dwellers in the Western world, who must find babysitters they can trust or raise the money to pay the neighborhood day-care center!

Generally it is agreed that children are taught the sex roles their culture describes as proper by observation and imitation of adult models, by work assignment, and by various forms of sanctions. This does not mean that children who are brought up together— for instance, mostly by their mother—necessarily will share all personality traits. Although there is but one Bonerate social system, Miang Tuu has as many personalities as there are villagers.

> However, there is an intimate relationship between social systems and personality: social systems operate by means of personality and personality functions by means of social systems. . . .
>
> Human social life demands that forms of social interaction, methods of social cooperation, techniques of conflict resolution and the like be learned. But this is not enough. Social existence is necessarily an orderly and regulated existence. Unless the members of a group are able to predict with some probability far greater than chance the behavior of other members of the group with whom they interact, social action, let alone interaction, would be all but precluded. (Spiro, 1961, p. 95)

Through socialization children acquire cultural values and goals that are usually disguised so that they appear to be personal rather than collective representations. Through childhood boys and girls learn which objects and events their culture permits them in order to reduce drives. Sex identity is an important part of the individual's self-identity. Socialization, as carried out in Miang Tuu, does not deny sex and sex-role differences even though few distinctions are drawn between what is regarded as proper conduct for boys and girls. Instead of a sex-role dichotomization, complementarity between the sexes is stressed in everyday interaction. When Miang Tuu boys do a great deal of "feminine" work and spend much time in company with women, different drives are often channelized by the same goals. Thus when a boy or his sister assist their mother at a task, they may well be satisfying different drives. However, a "feminine upbringing" of boys may still affect their personality development, and likewise the absence of the fathers will probably influence the development of girls, although differently from its effects on their brothers.

Mothers are assumed cross-culturally to identify differently with their sons and daughters. Through double identification, the mother reexperiences herself as a cared-for child. Because she was a girl herself and identification with her mother and mothering is strong, we may expect that a woman's identification with a girl might be stronger than her identification with a boy child. This would then lead the mother to treat infants of different sexes in different ways. This is in addition to different treatment due to the mother's amount of experience with child care, the household situation, and the temperament or other peculiarities of the infants (Chodorow, 1978). As a girl is growing up, her gender identification is primarily achieved through her mother. In Miang Tuu, the mother dyad is strong and lasting; it is a culturally positive relationship that is the focus of much village attention. The quality of this dyad creates a strong sense of gender and role identity in the girl. A son's case is different. On Bonerate also he is brought up to a large degree by women, but he perceives himself as different from them. He identifies with his father and other salient adult male villagers. These men are, however, relatively more remote and for extended periods of time inaccessible to the boy. As a result the boy's sex-role identity becomes a "positional" identification with aspects of his father's less clearly defined male role. His sister is likely to identify with a more total female role of her mother. Thus a boy is likely to define his masculinity in a negative way, in contrast to the sex of his omnipotent mother, by how he is different from her. Feminine identification is based on the gradual learning of a way of being familiar with household management exemplified by the person with whom the girl has been most involved. To the boy, masculinity becomes and remains a problematic issue. He must deny the dependence on his mother, he must repress or devaluate aspects of femininity, and he must search out male companions (Chodorow, 1974, pp. 43–46). In due time he must perhaps move to a strange village of many foreigners to marry.

If the "parent's anticipation of task performance in adulthood may affect social behavior acquisition in much the same way as differences in task assignment to children" (Ember, 1973, p. 437), this also, to some degree, legitimates the systematic delegation of household chores by mothers to their children of both sexes in Miang Tuu. Because the context of the task situation seems more critical than the task itself, it becomes somewhat misleading in the Bonerate context to mark most household work as female activity or to regard woodcutting or heavy agricultural labor as typical masculine work. To be a mother alone is as normal for a woman as it is for a young man to be a member of an all-male *perahu* crew. Like the "single" mother who must carry out much heavy work alone, the sailors have to prepare food and keep the vessel clean and tidy. If it is true that boys who do a great deal of "feminine work" (as defined by our Western culture) in the home are more "feminine" in their social behavior than boys who are not delegated such chores (Ember, 1973, pp. 432–433), Miang Tuu boys may be well prepared for a sailor's life. But it is just as important to recognize that the absence of fathers may provide daughters with both emotional and physical strength and qualities required of them in motherhood and often as major single providers. It seems highly functional in an island community such as Miang Tuu that few tasks are the business of the members of one sex only.

Socialization will always have to be accommodated to the economic and productive role of the caretakers. It is argued that the busy mother will be bossy and has little time to be permissive and indulgent. The busy mother expects and demands help from her children (Brown, 1973). This, of course, holds true as long as the mother is the only major caretaker. In Miang Tuu mothers are generally busy, but as we have seen the necessary help is available to tend their children while they are occupied with other things. This situation probably makes Bonerate mothers somewhat more permissive and indulgent than they would be if they had to tend their children continuously all by themselves along with their other work. The mother–child dyads in Bonerate social structure are also based on the idea of the ever-nurturant and indulgent mother figure. In societies where the mother–daughter dyad is the primary dyad, most ethnographies indicate that these same social facts make male development difficult. This is also true on Bonerate, but because the mother–son relation is another strong dyad, potential psychic conflicts may be strongly suppressed or hidden behind a lasting, overtly affectionate mother–son relationship. A boy cannot, for example, by verbal or other means offend his mother's position or question her authority. All social or personal rebellion in this context would immediately be negatively sanctioned by other villagers.

> A mother is not invested in keeping her daughter from individuating and becoming less dependent. She has other ongoing contacts and relationships that help fulfill her psychological and social needs. In addition, the people surrounding a mother while a child is growing up become mediators between mother and daughter, by providing a daughter with alternative models for personal identification and objects of attachment, which contribute to her differentiation from her mother. Finally, a daughter's identification with her mother in this kind of setting is with a strong woman with clear control over important spheres of life, whose sense of self-esteem can reflect this. Acceptance of her gender identity involves positive valuation of herself, and not admission of inferiority. (Chodorow, 1974, p. 63)

But also the Miang Tuu boy grows up in a world controlled to a large degree by his omnipotent mother. When he, for example, observes that his mother fails to collect fish from a weir because she says she cannot dive, this does not give added respect to his own sex. He knows that his father could have gathered the fish easily had he been home, but he also knows that several women in the village could have done so. It is not because his mother is a woman that she could not get the fish, but because her social position does not allow her to dive or even to swim. When the boy wants to understand what it is like to be a man, he cannot learn that from direct observation or identification with a father model to the same degree that his sister can identify with the mother. The boy has to practice his role in fantasy or in role play. Boys are also eager to go to sea to become sailors and through that experience achieve status as adult men (for more on male role conflict in boys, see the discussion of circumcision in Chapter 4). Overcompensation or exaggerated masculine behavior, which has been related to father absence elsewhere (Burton & Whiting, 1961), could not be observed in Miang Tuu. Masculine aggression, often seen among sailors in different parts of the world, is absent from Bonerate. The boys on the island have few models for adult aggressive behavior; the exceptions are the often rough conduct of the police and military personnel, who only rarely enter Miang Tuu and who, being strangers, would serve as negative role models (Broch, 1987).

Although direct practices enforced by a parent can shape the child's behavior, I have argued that to understand Miang Tuu child development we have to emphasize the household structure as an important element of the setting where the child learns about his role and identity. A prominent feature of Bonerate kinship is the mother–child and in particular the mother–daughter dyad. But we cannot hope to understand the child's development unless we also take into account his cognitive classification of others. The child is soon aware of his position within the village social structure and the way he acknowledges this will mold his attitude toward himself and others.

Leipi and Halimu

Leipi and Halimu, boys of approximately four and six years, were best friends, but their life situations differed remarkably. Leipi was the only son and youngest child of *ibu* and *kepala lingkung*. He had four older sisters and lived in the richest household in the village. His father stayed home and had a good reputation as an excellent *juragan* from earlier years. But now his two *perahus* were managed and sailed by his two sons-in-law. Leipi's father was a hard-working man, busily engaged in agricultural labor and skilled in fishing. Leipi's mother ran the household with a firm hand, assisted by her husband and her three oldest daughters, who also worked hard and demonstrated above-average skill in their undertakings. *Ibu* also occasionally organized additional work within the household carried out by other women in the village.

As will become clear, Leipi was in many ways a spoiled child, a fact that was recognized by his parents and other villagers. Leipi was never responsible for any duties and he was seldom asked for help by any household members. This was probably not so much due to his sex as to the fact that he was the youngest child in a large and, by local standards, affluent household. At home his cooperation and assistance in various tasks were in little demand. His two married sisters were almost as indulgent to him as his mother and father were. His youngest sister was too close to him in age to enforce her authority upon him. The few times she tried she was told to submit to her little brother's wishes; this resulted in conflicts of envy and the two seldom played together. Only his sister Haisa, who was approximately fifteen years old, occasionally was successful in restricting his spoiled behavior. But generally this behavior on her part was negatively sanctioned. Within the household she was often teased for being too emotional, angry, and impatient. There were, however, limitations to what Leipi could achieve by pouting and crying. One day it was decided that there were too many lice in the hair of both Halimu and Leipi. Halimu was sent home, where his grandmother cut off all his hair, which was the best way to get rid of the unwanted insects. He did not resist the decision and shortly returned bald-headed. Although a little timid, he smiled and watched his friend's rather hysterical resistance. Leipi cried and kicked his mother while he demanded to be spared. But that day nothing could help him. His father grabbed the scissors and cut off the hair, leaving only a tuft close to the front of the boy's head. A little while later the two boys left the house, their common destiny apparently comforting them.

Halimu was the oldest son of his mother; his father had died at sea before his baby sister was born. Halimu grew up with his mother and mother's mother, who shared a tiny hut in the village. Their household was among the poorest in the village. Some nights Halimu spent at home, but usually he slept with other villagers, and most often he spent his time in the household of *kepala lingkung*. His father had been a crew member on one of *kepala*'s *perahus*. Therefore, *kepala* said, he felt responsible for Halimu, his mother, and his grandmother. Halimu was not adopted by *kepala,* but he helped out with many minor tasks, such as fetching water and bringing home forgotten tools from various places. He was an ever-present playmate of Leipi. At night they often slept side by side, but when Leipi ate supper with his father and the anthropologist, Halimu ate with the women. In that way the different status of the two boys was explicitly expressed.

Because Halimu grew up partly in the *kepala lingkung* household, he had to learn that his status was different from his best friend Leipi. The two boys were not equals. Halimu was asked for help in far more instances than his friend. When Halimu stayed home, he was busy helping his mother and grandmother in weeding, harvesting cassava, fetching water, and collecting sea urchins. One evening when all the children of the household were home, *kepala* found that he forgot his soap bar at the well. He called for Halimu. The boy did not respond to his call immediately, so *kepala* interrogated others to see what he was up to. When he found him, he asked Halimu to get the soap for him. Still, Halimu had more time for leisure in the household of *kepala lingkung* than he had at home.

One night Halimu went to sleep close to Leipi. Both had their sleeping mats on the floor in the living room. When *kepala* was ready to go to sleep, he observed that Halimu was lying close by a fragile cupboard's glass door. He gently lifted the boy up and moved him further away from the glass door. *Kepala* explained, "He is no good, this boy! He kicks and hits while asleep." And this was true; Halimu often woke up all the other household members when he shouted and cried during his frequent nightmares. Nobody in the village was willing to guess why Halimu was so often plagued by nightmares.

Halimu received many goodies, but not as many nor as often as Leipi. Often Halimu was dependent on Leipi's moods and willingness to share. But because Halimu was smart he also took advantage of his environment and asked Leipi to grab or demand things that he himself wanted from the house. Thus Leipi often pretended temper tantrums to get such goodies as cigarettes. When Leipi got what he wanted the boys soon left the house to smoke openly in the village. Halimu usually got the butts! Although Leipi often pouted or threw tantrums if he did not get what he wanted quickly, Halimu was never observed to behave that way. When he was asked to do something, he always did what he was told. To some degree his mother and grandmother depended on him, because they too received food and other favors for Halimu's services. Besides this, they also often worked for *ibu* in the *kepala* household. *Ibu* and *bapak lingkung* were kind to Halimu. They did not demand too much from him, in the opinion of the villagers. They favored him with things most other village children were without. They bought him new clothes and also brought him along as a playmate for Leipi on a voyage to Java. But Halimu was never treated as a son. His social status was clearly different from that of their own children. Thus his behavior and the way he was treated served as a model to demonstrate the importance of social position to rich and poor villagers alike.

To small boys, smoking is a marker of status. The act may in the Miang Tuu context signify both maturity and success, because emically it is regarded as "normal abnormal" behavior in small boys. It is not because of the health risk that youngsters should not smoke—that hazard is not seriously acknowledged. Rather, children should not smoke because tobacco is expensive and not to be enjoyed by economically unproductive members of the society. Thus, not alone the act of smoking, but also the amount of the tobacco put into the homemade cigarettes or the brand of cigarette smoked signifies the socioeconomic status of the smoker. When Leipi obtained cigarettes that he shared with Halimu, they both appeared rather proud and self-confident. The two boys often took up positions in front of a mirror when they smoked. There they smiled and let the smoke out of their small noses. Other times they paraded through the village, puffing their cigarettes to the envy of other small boys, and even to the envy of adults, both men and women. Because smoking was not regarded as bad in itself, no one sanctioned their behavior negatively. Instead adults and adolescents smiled at them, thereby confirming the privileges of the rich child and his faithful friend! Even when Halimu was left with only the butts, he was fortunate compared to other small boys in the village who did not receive similar favors from Leipi. Halimu, being a close friend of Leipi and under the protection of the *kepala lingkung* household, was privileged to act according to a borrowed status that was very much like being a friend and at the same time a small servant. At home Halimu had to share what he got; only when with Leipi or inside the house of *ibu lingkung* was he free to enjoy these special privileges. Thus he at an early age was taught the importance of friendship and obedience to the rich to improving his material consumption. Also the relationship served as a model to other young and older villagers. As we shall see, this pattern of interaction across social borders is explicitly repeated in the relationship between Leipi's youngest sister Owati and her best girlfriend. This type of relationship, as would be expected, endures into and is duplicated in adult interaction.

Leipi begged not only cigarettes from his father, but also, and often at the initiative of Halimu, money from his mother. When his wish was granted, as was usually the case, the two of them immediately spent it on village-made goodies. If Halimu understood the importance of his friendship with Leipi in a pragmatic way, the latter also took advantage of the structure of the situation. At times he would make Halimu do things for him, and sometimes he would not share his treasures or best food with Halimu. Leipi was not encouraged by his parents to share everything with Halimu. But it would be unthinkable for Halimu not to share what he ate in front of Leipi, if Leipi wanted to taste it.

I once brought home some bananas. Leipi, who was playing inside with Halimu, demanded a banana. When I made it clear that Halimu should also have one, both Leipi's parents shook their heads and asked why I should also give one to Halimu.

At this early age, Leipi and Halimu recognized that the same rules do not apply to them both in many daily aspects of village life. And the two of them adjusted to this feature of their social environment. When Leipi sat smoking in a chair, Halimu sat on the floor, also smoking or waiting for the butt!

In Bonerate culture, a characteristic trait that is enforced in many different ways is that everyone must know her or his social position and must pay the respect due to those above by submissive behavior and controlled lip service. All Miang Tuu children observe their parents acting out such servile roles in some contexts. However, they also learn that their parents feel frustrated in this behavior, but that this frustration cannot be articulated within the interactional context that creates it. The frustration can only be aired in a "backstage" setting.[3] Within the household or among equals, frustration due to social inequality is often bitterly or fatalistically commented on. The lesson repeatedly learned from such encounters by both youngster and adult seems to be that the situa-

---

[3] *Backstage* here refers to a dramaturgical model of action (Goffman, 1959).

tion has to be exploited to the best of one's ability. The power structure that maintains social inequality is regarded as so strong that any resistance to the rules of behavior in this interaction will prove disastrous to the weaker person. By the time children reach maturity, it is as important for them to know their social position as to control their emotions (see the discussion in the section A Closer Look at Circumcision Rituals in Chapter 4). These closely related social skills are required to obtain adult status.

Children in Play

Play and play activities are concepts that are easy to describe and yet hard to define. When people describe an activity they also categorize it, and when they act according to the description they do so with reference to the categories. For analytical purposes play has been categorized and described in various ways, depending on the purpose of the investigation. So far no definition of play has gained broad acceptance within the social sciences. Focus has been put on play development, diffusion, or play as a means through which social values and skills are achieved. From a purely psychological point of view, play has been seen to function in childhood to release pent-up emotions and to give imaginary relief for past frustrations.

> Another, plausible explanation was that the child utilized the increasing mastery over toys for playful arrangements that permitted the illusion of also mastering some pressing life predicaments. For Freud, play, above all, turned enforced passivity into imaginary activity. (Erikson, 1982, p. 59)

To Bonerate islanders, as perhaps to most of us, play is a kind of borderline phenomenon to a number of human activities. Play can become work, and work can become play. Both young children and the oldest villagers may join in play. Play is in Miang Tuu emically defined by the context in which the activity takes place rather than by the activity itself. Play is defined in opposition to work. Although adults may play, they work most of their time. While, by emic definition, children mostly play, they also help in their parents' work. Still, the contribution of children is not regarded as quite serious and necessary work. When children help their parents they are not really working, but they are not really playing either. On this issue children and parents often disagree. Among the activities children classify as work is helping their parents. Both parents and children see pure amusement and make-believe activities as play. Both young and old seem to agree that play is what one does with the time left over from working and resting. Miang Tuu children have more time available to play than most Western children today, because they do not attend schools and their parents do not force too many assignments on them.

In the description and analyses of play that follow, I use the emic definition of play by following the adult's view without completely ignoring the children's perception of their own activities. I shall focus less on material aspects of play and more on social and psychological functions of the activities. For the purpose of the analysis, I have categorized types of play into overlapping rather than finite groups. I have labeled one of these categories *gamelike play.* The others are imitation play, fantasy play, role play, and unstructured play. While play is a cultural universal, games are not; games are found in most societies but are absent in a few. To verify this observation, games have been

> defined as a recreational activity characterized by (1) organized play, (2) competition, (3) two or more sides, (4) criteria for determining the winner, and (5) agreed-upon rules. (Roberts, Arth, & Bush, 1959, p. 597)

Because no play activities observed among Miang Tuu children fulfill all the elements of the above definition, I shall refrain from calling any play in the village a game. Because some play activities do, however, resemble games by lacking only one or two elements of this definition, I shall refer to them as gamelike play.

If we compare the play of Miang Tuu children with the play of children from many other cultures, some features are at once striking. Miang Tuu play is generally noncompetitive, winners are not singled out, and there is little or no emphasis on better or worse performances. True games are absent. Imaginary or fantasy play is poorly developed, and play activities involving imitation of adult occupations are few. Girls and boys have almost no toys; they never play with dolls or toy cars. Aggression is seldom expressed explicitly during play, except when children amuse themselves with animals.

One theme commonly elaborated in play activities in Miang

Tuu is different ways to handle emotional control. Children seldom withdraw from play because they are not doing well, get hurt, or disagree on rules. As we shall see, both aggressive and affectionate needs can find outlet through play under cover of emotional control and the play context.

Composition of Play Groups

Play groups in Miang Tuu vary in both composition and number of participants from instance to instance. It is impossible to single out a particular model play group. Generally girls and boys play together, and children of different ages mix freely. However, young boys tend to seek out the company of somewhat older girls. Play groups may occasionally be all male or all female, usually when dyadic or other small groups are formed. The size of groups is most importantly related to the whereabouts of the village children. Because some activities cannot be combined with child tending and other assignments, these tasks may divide the players into different groups. Some will play at locations or engage in activities the child tenders cannot join because of their primary duty. The latter may then form their own group and engage in docile play such as throwing "marbles." Miang Tuu children are rarely observed to play alone. They always seek out the company of others. There is little difference in role taking when we compare girls with boys, although some differences can be observed, especially in emotional expression during play.

Socially ascribed position, seems to have more relevance in play leadership than physical skills and general maturity. Some children more often inaugurate play activities than do others. Although it would be false to speak about these children as dominant or true leaders, they often color the play by their influence. Their leadership is not strict in the sense that they can boss other children around or force reluctant playmates into activities. The atmosphere of all Miang Tuu play is warm and friendly, but the personal resources of the children differ. Some children are stronger or more courageous and some can climb higher, run faster, and swim better than the rest. These skills are of course shown during play. But the resources that are most important in many play contexts are the social and material resources that are also unevenly distributed among the children of the different village households.

The social resources generally derive from the social status of the child's parents. The respect all villagers pay to *ibu* and *bapak lingkung*, for instance, is partly transferred to their children. Material resources are linked to social position. The more affluent households are able to provide their children with more play materials, such as *kemiri* nuts, sewing thread, fishing line, and empty boxes. These are objects other children do not have access to unless they borrow them from the more fortunate ones during play. Thus, social and material resources are manipulated by some children to support their diffuse leadership role among their peers. A last personal resource, of equal importance in this context, is the intelligence of the child. *Intelligence* is here demonstrated by the child's ability to "analyze" the play situation in order to control it and, further, the child's ability (for instance, by verbal skills) to maintain or change the play according to his or her own interests. Social position is the one most important personal identity marker and resource a Miang Tuu child brings along to any play or other social encounter. We see that children of the most affluent households repeatedly can inaugurate new play activities after they have just failed to maintain leadership through the previous activity. But how one manipulates resources once they are controlled is important in becoming a leader. All children of relatively equal socioeconomic status do not become play leaders, even in the diffuse meaning of leadership used here. Sex is of little importance in the recruitment of play leaders. Both boys and girls may take on that role when they play together. During my stay in Miang Tuu, the child who inaugurated most play activities and showed the most initiative and creativity was a girl of approximately eleven years, the youngest daughter of *bapak* and *ibu lingkung*. Because the sample is limited, that this girl was the "most dominant" at the time does not mean that girls usually hold that position. She was the right age, among the eldest who were regularly playing, and she was also a bright child. It is not possible to predict that another girl will take over her position. When she gradually stops playing, there might not be anybody, girl or boy, of her caliber to fill her position.[4]

---

[4] Further information on this girl, Owati, and her role among her peers is presented later in this chapter.

Everyday Play Activities

Most play activities can be viewed as serving the development of the personal and social skills that are important in adult community life. Play is, in other words, a significant element in the socialization of all children. In Western societies we are so concerned about our childrens' play that we discuss "right" toys and forms of play. This would imply that we also have clear ideas about which toys and play activities are wrong for the healthful development of our children.

Bonerate parents are not much concerned about how their children play. They rarely direct or stage play activities for their children and seldom make or find toys for them. Their notion of "bad play" would be what they regard as dangerous play, and they try to keep their youngest children from such activities as paddling dugouts or climbing tall coconut palms. Adults have their own games—card games, competitive war dances (Broch, 1984), and cockfights—in which children are not allowed to participate. Adults seldom join children in their play. This noninvolvement of Miang Tuu parents does not mean that they do not understand or reflect upon the developmental potential of many play activities. Adults sometimes comment on physical and other skills that children develop and display through their various activities, and they may refer to the need for such skills in adult life. However, parents never propose to a child that she or he should play this or that. This may appear strange to Westerners when we remember that Miang Tuu children do not attend schools. However, children are allowed to participate in some adult work when they want to join their parents. Children must be free to choose what they want to do and in due time they will be prepared for adult life and work, the villagers say. In Miang Tuu children were never observed to complain of having nothing to do or to seek advice from their parents with regard to play activities.

Children, of course, do not consciously choose play activities to prepare themselves for adult life. However, they may choose to role play, or imitate social situations from which children are barred. Thus what they cannot do in real life children can do in play. The educational aspects of such play are obvious, but play activities are multifunctional. Not only does play fulfill the development of various skills and roles, but it may also respond to more personal exhibitionistic or narcissistic needs, such as nurturance, suppressed aggression, or relief from anxiety. What has a common meaning to all playing children, and perhaps to watching adults, may have a special meaning to some. Play symbols may be both collective and personal symbols at the same time. Although of necessity we must analyze play activities at one level at a time, we must also keep in mind the multiplex nature of play. We cannot reveal all aspects important to our understanding of play activities with reference to both social and psychological variables. The interpretation of personal symbols would be especially difficult, because it would require data not available in the Miang Tuu case. This much said, we can turn to the ethnography of Bonerate play.

Much Miang Tuu play resembles the description of Manus children who, unaided by the rich hints for play that children of other societies take from admired adult traditions, are carelessly playing about. The play of Manus children is like that of young puppies or kittens, romping good-humoredly until they are tired, then lying inert and breathless until rested sufficiently to romp again (Mead, 1975, p. 8). Miang Tuu children love to play on the beach and in the water where they swim, dive, and splash water at each other. Boys and girls mingle freely, most of them naked. But some, especially the older girls (from nine to twelve years old) who have been circumcised, wear skirts or *sarongs*. However, they are not apparently bothered if and when the *sarong* is torn off or loosens by itself during play. But when the girls return to the shore, they wrap themselves tightly in the soaking wet *sarongs*.

Sometimes a dugout canoe may be the center of play. It is like a castle that has to be held against intruders who are thrown into the water when they try to get on board. Quite often the canoe capsizes and the defenders and intruders all fall in the water. This play never becomes violent. If after a while the intruders do not manage to throw the defenders into the sea, the latter jump into the water voluntarily.[5]

Play is often quite unstructured. Most Bonerate days are hot and sunny, but as soon as a heavy rainshower drains the village,

---

[5] The terminology used to describe this play is that of the Western anthropologist attempting to make sense of the activity. The children do not speak about attackers, intruders, or defenders; they simply play in the water and try to get on board the canoe.

most young children gather naked outside to run up and down between the houses. They shout and scream and run and jump into the pools while the rainwater splashes high into the air. Boys and girls are together, throwing water at each other. Those who did not have the time to take off their clothes will soon be thoroughly wet to the skin. Now and then the children pause for a moment. Against the cold, they press their small arms to their chests. But soon they are on the run again. Their parents watch them from inside, where they too are freezing in spite of extra *sarongs*. The children carry on the play until completely exhausted; only then do they return home shivering cold.

I have mentioned that there are few toys for the children to play with. But there are exceptions. With the help from older friends or adults, boys sometimes make small boats they sail in the lagoon. The boats are miniature *perahus* and outrigger canoes equipped with sails. The *perahus* are made from unripened coconuts, the outriggers from bamboo, and the sails usually from plastic. The boats make good speed in the breeze and the boys run or swim beside them. Girls occasionally join in, but usually only boys engage in this activity.

Only toddlers are much involved in symbolic play in the sense that they substitute imaginary objects for material ones. The boats the boys play with are replicas of models. The toddlers, however, may stroll along with a stick or an empty box tied to the end of a string, playing that they are handling a horse, a dog, or a chicken (these are their parents' interpretations of the activity). But perhaps the toddler, at another and deeper level, may identify with both the object being pulled and the object that pulls. If this is so, he may imitate the situation he so often experiences while being led around the village, hand in hand with a child tender. This play activity may give the toddler a feeling of control.

As the toddlers grow, they become dissatisfied with this make-believe play. Children's pretending to be a fierce animal such as a shark or a tiger, which is so common in other societies, was never observed in Miang Tuu.

One day a boy of approximately eight years attracted the attention of most other children his age and younger in the village. He had soapy water in a coconut shell and blew soap bubbles with a bamboo pipe. None of the other children was allowed to borrow soap, water, or pipe to blow bubbles, but they gathered to cheer each bubble that appeared. They also expressed dissatisfaction when it burst, in spite of their combined efforts to break all the soap bubbles as fast as possible by touching them.

Playing with "marbles" is another popular activity in the village that involves the use of toys. Although this activity resembles a game in many ways, it does not quite satisfy the definition of games referred to earlier. In Miang Tuu no children own real marbles; they do know what marbles look like because most of them have seen the real thing in the *ibu kota*. But there are two good substitutes for marbles: marine mollusk shells and *kemiri* nuts. The shells are easily found and gathered in large numbers along the shore in front of the village. *Kemiri* nuts, which have a better shape for playing, are in short demand and only a few children have access to them. Thus, the nuts have to be distributed before and often redistributed during play. In both instances, whether one plays with shells or *kemiri* nuts, it seems to make little sense for the children to name a winner. With the shells nobody is able to play a coplayer empty, and with *kemiri* nuts the play would stop too soon if the nuts were not redistributed several times during play. When the play is ended all nuts are returned to their original owners. When Miang Tuu children play marbles they often disagree on the rules for playing. There are several ways of playing marbles in Miang Tuu and there is creativity in the variation and complexity of the rules. One of the two most frequent methods is to throw the marbles, one at the time, as close as possible to a line, a stick, or another object. In the second method, every participant deposits one marble close to the center of a circle drawn in the sand. Then the participants each in turn try to throw marbles into the circle in order to push those already deposited there outside the boundary marked by the circle. In this activity Miang Tuu children imitate games played in the *ibu kota,* Bonerate. There the rules are fixed and the children win and lose real marbles, and no substitutes are accepted. In Miang Tuu boys and girls play with marbles in mixed groups, while in *ibu kota* children tend to divide into a boys' and a girls' group for marble games.

In Miang Tuu three girls were outstanding experts with marbles; they never won objects from their playmates, but they were the ones who most often tried to start "marble play" in the village. It seems obvious that these girls gained some personal satisfaction by their demonstration of competence. Some other children tried to compensate for their lack in skill by cheating in various ways. They could try to throw two marbles at one time, then they would claim that the marble closest to the line actually was theirs (*kemiri* nuts all look much the same), or they would fall or stumble so the marbles were all scattered. The cheaters were not barred from continuous play, and usually their tricks were as far as possible ignored. When an argument started, it was usually between the second and third bests and the cheaters; the experts seldom got involved in these disputes that threatened to stop the activity.

Another gamelike activity is a play of chance. One participant hides a string with a small loop at the end beneath some sand. Each of the other children has a tiny stick that they force into the sand, trying to penetrate the sand right through the loop. The string is then pulled free and if a stick has reached its goal, the owner of that stick is allowed to hit the one who hid the loop. The blow has to be struck with the same stick that was used to locate the loop. This is lots of fun. Both boys and girls participate, although girls are more eager and seem to enjoy this play more than boys do. Lots of laughter always accompanies this activity; the blows handed out are never hard. Although I have no evidence to claim so, this play could easily be interpreted as relating to primary sexual wish fulfillment of the children. Children are well aware of sexuality, but overt sexual play or experimentation is not tolerated by Bonerate culture. Also adult villagers enjoy watching this play in the sand. Often they seem to find it even funnier than the players themselves. They could not or perhaps would not explain their reactions. They had no other explanation than that they found it very funny and seemed puzzled about my questions of how or why this particular play activity was so amusing to watch.

The most aggressive play I observed in Miang Tuu (except for play with some animals) lasted for two days and was not to be seen before or after that time. The play involved all boys between the ages of four and eleven and it generated lots of excitement. The boys divided themselves into two parties, although the membership of each group was rather unstable. Each party or group lost members and gained new ones as boys switched sides all the time. The boys were fighting each other, using their fists and sometimes open hands. Often boys were thrown quite roughly onto the ground during the combat. But the fights were not without some kind of order and style. The boys imitated adult Bonerate male war dancers with their highly stylized movements. Sometimes a boy would assume a dramatically threatening pose and suddenly throw a fist at high speed towards a playmate of the opposite group. But the terrible blow froze about an inch or so from the target. Usually the harder blows and those aimed at the face of the counterpart were frozen just like those of war dancers in their shadow fights.[6] I watched this play as it rolled back and forth for almost the entire two days. As it progressed the play sometimes appeared quite violent; I became more and more astonished that no one got hurt or cried! One of Western origin would suspect the play to end with a little boy running home crying, especially considering the great age differences among the combatants. No girl participated in this war, which the boys called their play. But the girls all watched the wild performance from the sideline and cheered and applauded heartily.

This "war play" is interesting for several reasons. The play is very physical, but speed, strength, and aggression are remarkably controlled for the age of the participants. The boys are never carried away by the obvious excitement generated and experienced during the play. This is one of the few sex-bound activities in which girls do not participate. This is in harmony with the model for the play, the adult war dances. That these adult dances are never staged in Miang Tuu may partly explain the very free imitation of the child actors. I have witnessed boys in the *ibu kota* in similar play. Those boys followed the war dance pattern more strictly than Miang Tuu children do. In *ibu kota* real war dances are often staged and the children there are thus quite familiar with the rules and stylized movements.

I believe that during this play Miang Tuu boys experience a sense of sex identity by being warriors and engaging in a restricted male activity. This feeling of male identity is strengthened by their fantasies, which reach beyond a restricted social dance context. During play children repeat things that have made a great impression on them in real life and put themselves in a position where they can master the situation (Freud, 1961). In this case, the children express male behavior in accordance with their fantasies of

---

[6] Semai boys in Malaya engage in a similar play, but that is explained with reference to parental gestures of aggression toward their children (see Dentan, 1978).

maleness. The basis for these fantasies is not primarily found in everyday village life, but in the stories men sometimes tell of daring voyages, times of war, and warlike fights. Fierce behavior is denied the children in most everyday settings other than this play. The boys may also find gratification for many pent-up aggressive feelings, if such feelings indeed are present, that can be played out both in fairly disguised and more explicit ways by attacking playmates. It is of course also possible to project aggressive feelings onto objects that are justified targets of "hostility" within the play context. The important social lesson learned here is emotional control "during the heat of war." Not only is the physical combat controlled, but even when some boys received a fairly hard blow, they did not cry. In other contexts I observed young boys to cry when they accidentally got hit by what appeared to be less forceful blows than those some experienced here. The adults who watched this play did not intervene. During other circumstances, aggression and even tentative aggressive display between children is immediately frowned upon. All Miang Tuu boys between four and eleven years participated, although they were not all equally involved in the brawls. Some boys were more active fighters while others merely ran on the heels of their strongest peers. Thus some got the satisfaction of rough fighting and others of being protectors of younger boys; still others were protected and got the thrill of being in the middle of the battle without really being physically involved! An intriguing aspect of the play was that it was not so much a fight or competition between two sides as a play of continuous war. As soon as one side seemed to be stronger than the other, the alliances were adjusted to equal the relative strength of the sides. Thus the purpose of the play was not to make a winning team, but to continue the war!

Once I observed five girls engaged in the imitation of a female possession-trance ritual (see Broch, 1985a). The girls, all between four and seven years of age, were dancing and acting out the various roles of the ritual experts. They put the most elaboration into the act of walking on or stamping out imaginary embers. This play took place just a few days after a real possession-trance ritual had been conducted in a neighboring village. In their play the girls were training themselves for an exclusive female skill, as only women are thought to have the ability to kill live embers in a state of trance. According to the villagers, all men would be seriously burned if they were to try. The girls' imitation was interesting because the villagers were emotionally concerned and divided about the moral and religious legitimation of possession-trance rituals. A significant number of the villagers disapproved of this ritual because of the way it violates and opposes their notions of Muslim faith. These villagers claimed in conversation with me that only old islanders participated in the ritual. The play of the girls, however, proved that they had indeed been present during possession-trance rituals, and that they were excited about what they had experienced. The children of the household in which I lived, were not only forbidden to watch the ritual, but they were also not allowed to play possession-trancers. I believe such incidents to be important to the development of ego identity of the children. Here they are taught quite explicitly that some can do things, and they participate in activities that others are barred from. Individuals are different, and religious beliefs also separate as well as bind families, households, and individuals. Differences in options to behavior must be explicit at a very early age in a small village such as Miang Tuu where everybody knows everybody and has extensive information on what all are doing most of the time.

Let us now return to the problem of role taking in children.

> A child's imitation of someone with whom he interacts may properly be called "taking the role of another" only if the action imitated is inappropriate for a child, and is appropriate instead for the occupants of some other position or status. (Maccoby, 1959, p. 242)

Although the possession-trance imitators demonstrate role taking during play, this is a form of play that is indeed little developed among Miang Tuu children. I shall, however, give another example of such play before discussing why role taking may be of so little concern to the children in the village.

Owati, an eleven-year-old girl who was in the center of many play activities, had one strong wish for her future. She wanted to open a small shop in the village. To this day no shops had been operated in the village, but the girl had often visited several in the *ibu kota*. Her dream was not really unrealistic. She would need money to get started, but as the youngest daughter of *ibu* and *bapak lingkung,* she might be able to obtain that capital. Still, many years would have to pass before her dream could come true.

Meanwhile, Owati opened a play shop in the shade below the floor of her home. She made a counter on which she displayed her large variety of goods for "sale." She gathered sea shells and wrapped sand in banana leaves; she had *kemiri* nuts, empty boxes, and packets of cigarettes refilled with tiny sticks. She never switched roles and let her friends run the shop. Owati was always in charge of her shop. She might occasionally "hire" assistants to carry out odd jobs, such as gathering new supplies for her display. But Owati never wanted to play the customer role; that role was reserved for her friends. Sometimes she was busy and small customers, both boys and girls, came to her shop to "buy" and chat. But often Owati sat alone behind her counter. I asked her if she liked to sit alone like that when her playmates were engaged in other activities. She responded that business was up and down, but that her customers would surely return! No other child put up a shop during my stay in Miang Tuu. I think the case neatly illustrates how personal needs can be integrated in play. To the other children her shop was just another creation of Owati, who often inaugurated play activities. They joined her as customers and did not protest her role delegations. This contrasts with observations in a Norwegian kindergarten where girls also liked to play shopkeeper and customers. But when the Norwegian girls played shop, they ran into severe difficulties in deciding who should be in charge. In other words, it was difficult for them to create a social situation. In the kindergarten a difference emerged between the play of boys and girls that is absent in Miang Tuu. In the Norwegian context girl leaders never managed to establish themselves, but the boys quickly chose leaders. When girls started to play, they did not agree on a social position that gave any girl a means of sanctions to direct and shape the activity at her own will (Berentzen, 1980). In Miang Tuu, Owati managed to stage her play according to her own rules. The activity surely gave her some wish fulfillment, as she had her own shop that attracted customers. Several other issues were underlined by Owati's activities. Owati put herself in a special position by not allowing others to act her role. To the other children that was quite natural, because she was the privileged daughter of *kepala lingkung* and thus was entitled to special treatment. The play setting also revealed differences in the basis and potential for role identification. To Owati it was natural to be the shop owner, and the other children might well wish more strongly to be able to afford to enter a shop and buy goods than to own a shop. Most Miang Tuu children never had the opportunity to go shopping in real life; even their parents seldom could afford to do that. It is not then farfetched to propose that Owati's primary needs for grandiosity were given some gratification within a socially accepted play context.

Many Miang Tuu child activities resemble imitation play. Both boys and girls almost daily build small fireplaces on which they roast seashore snacks. We could perhaps interpret this as household imitation play. Gender roles during the play are diffuse, but so are they also in many aspects of adult life, or outside what can be properly called a play context. The children make their own small meals when they are hungry. From a nutritional point of view, their snacking is surely important. Bonerate diet is periodically remarkably poor in proteins. During these periods the children receive a better protein supply than adult villagers because of the larger amounts of bivalves, marine worms, and mollusks the children eat outside the household setting. It is my interpretation, then, that this is not a make-believe activity, but that the children prepare real food because they are hungry.

The paucity of imitation play in Miang Tuu could be due to the fact that the children themselves do most things their parents do for real. Dream-wishes like Owati's are too few or atypical to trigger and inspire much play creativity. Miang Tuu children have little need or desire to play with dolls or to play mother, father, and child. Bonerate children are integrated into many daily household chores; they look after live babies and toddlers. Dolls would not gratify understimulated needs in this context. Also, instead of playing agriculturally influenced activities, the children, at will and for as long as they want, may usually join their parents. To the children it does not matter whether their parents say they are playing when they run about or even complicate fishing for the adults. The child feels he or she is doing the real thing, helping the parents in existentially important tasks. Compare this situation to the setting in most Western societies where children are regarded as a hindrance to much adult work and have to remain at a distance. In Western societies work opportunities seem so many and the future holds an enormous variety of job possibilities that can be imitated in children's play. Miang Tuu children feel confident knowing that, when they themselves come of age, they will be doing what their parents do now. Thus far no television or other idea-stimulating or dream-provoking stimuli have reached the community.

Before we turn to children and their relationship with animals, I shall give another example of a typical Miang Tuu child activity. It can hardly be termed play, although it fills up leisure time. Bodily contact and expression of emotion are not frequently observed on Bonerate. However, one activity that girls often engage in contains both these elements. When the children have been playing physically for some time, or when they otherwise want to rest, girls often form a circle. They may sit cross-legged or stand close behind one other. For a while they will groom one another's hair. Every girl comforts the one standing or sitting just in front of her. Thus, each one is groomed by the girl behind and is grooming the one in front of her. This grooming is also a hunt for lice. Every insect is killed on the spot. I have never seen boys form such circles or join the girls. Grooming is regarded as a private affair in most contexts. A wife may groom her husband, and rarely a husband may do the same for his wife. However, wives also refuse to groom their men to express their dissatisfaction or anger with them. Adults never groom each other in public—that is, outside the house or in the presence of visitors. Women groom each other, but I have not heard of men doing the same. Usually the mother, but sometimes the father, grooms the hair of a young son or daughter, often at the child's bedtime.

The girl circles may well be interpreted as a cultural expression of the importance placed on female nurturance or of the mothering potential and responsibilities of girls. The activity may also express the social relevance and importance of an emerging female solidarity. The situation further suggests that the restraints on emotional expression, at least in some nurturant contexts, are somewhat less thorough in the case of girls and women than for boys and men.

Children and Animals

Most Westerners would be repelled by many of the ways Miang Tuu villagers treat animals, including the ways children play with or sometimes "torture" animals. However, the notion of cruelty, especially to lower animals such as insects, fish, and even birds, would never occur to the Bonerate islander.[7]

Young children often catch insects and birds, keep them tied to strings, and play with them before they eventually kill them during play. Children are never checked when they maltreat animals. Instead their play is often encouraged by the comments and laughter of their parents and other adult villagers. This behavior is regarded a natural interest of children and not a moral problem; in fact, adults find it entertaining to watch. Domesticated animals such as poultry, cats, dogs, and horses are somewhat better off. They are not treated with great affection but, because of their economic and food value, their lives are usually spared.

It is quite noteworthy that in the Bonerate culture, which offers so few santioned outlets for aggressive behavior, children's play with animals seems to provide an aggressive gratification to both the young actors and the adult onlookers. I shall return later to the aggressive elements in much of children's relationships with animals, but first I present some examples as a basis for the discussion.

The nature of child–animal relations varies with the age of children, the particular child, and the animal species involved. When the youngest children have pet chickens, the birds die of unintended maltreatment. The toddler does not kill the pet on purpose. The child is still too young to control the strength and force of movements, and when tired of the play he ignores the pet and does not feel responsible for its well-being. The young child is too egocentric to feel true nurturance toward objects outside himself. When the pet dies because of harsh treatment or neglect, the child may express sadness because the pet failed to be alive to amuse him. The death of the tiny bird was an accident experienced by the child as quite unrelated to his own actions. This is very different from the behavior of older children in play with animals, when a part of the entertainment provided by animals is their death. The desperate sorrow often observed in many Western cultures when pets die is not seen in Miang Tuu. For instance, children never

---

[7] Similar attitudes exist among Europeans. Respect for animal life does not extend to flies and mosquitoes but sometimes to butterflies. Animals such as wolves, bears, and lynx are often hated for the harm they do and might do.

think of staging "funerals" for their dead pets as Western children often do. In Miang Tuu it is unthinkable that a child or anybody else would cry at the death of a pet. Crying at death is ritually pre-scribed but restricted to the death of humans. This could lead us to speculate about whether we in our societies tend to project more human feelings into our pets than the Bonerate islanders generally do. On Bonerate nurturance and affectionate care is directed only —but at the same time generously—to young humans and not to tender animals as well.

From the approximate age of four up to thirteen years or so, children treat animals more and more roughly. After around the age of seven, girls take less direct part in "cruelties" towards ani-mals than boys do. But like adults girls also love to watch when older boys play with animals. Adults stress the play aspects less than children when they act aggressively towards animals. Adults may kick a cat or a dog once or twice quite hard, or kill a monkey or poisonous fish with a single blow of the *parang,* but adults sel-dom torture animals for prolonged periods as older boys like to do.

When crickets are plentiful the villagers take it as a sign that the rainy season is close. But to the children the crickets first of all provide sought-after play objects. All day long boys and girls (from five to ten years old) hunt them down from the coconut palm's trunks, using cone-shaped pieces of paper or banana plant leaves attached to long bamboo poles. The trick is to make the cricket fall into the cone, from which it is seldom able to escape. When the insect is caught it is handled carefully until it produces a chirping sound. That is the last thing it does, because after it has "sung that song" it is grabbed and the legs are torn off. Then it is dropped down to the ground, where it is watched for a brief moment before it is killed. Then the hunt continues until another cricket is located. As soon as one is caught the lucky catcher yells out to inform the other children who immediately come running to watch the fun.

A similar entertaining play by children of the same age is carried out with butterflies. The insects are first captured, then tied to a long sewing thread and let loose to fly while the child holds on to the other end of the thread. The butterfly is pulled down and let loose in the same way one would operate a kite. Sometimes two butterflies are caught and tied to the opposite ends of the thread before they are let loose. To make it possible for the youngest children to participate in this play, their older peers or sometimes their parents help them to attach the insect to the thread. After a while, when the butterfly is tired and does not fly readily, it is recaptured, the wings are torn off, and it is finally killed. A butterfly is never released but is always molested and killed.

A third activity involving insects is carried out by boys and girls around ten years old. Locusts are captured, tied to a string, and made to move in front of a duck. The bird, though fairly slow in its movements, usually tries to grab and eat the locust. The purpose of the play is to see how close the duck can get before the insect is pulled away from the bird. The play ends either when the duck manages to eat the locust, or when the insect refuses to move. In the latter case the locust is smashed and not given to the duck!

When captured by boys above the age of eight, poisonous fish and fish carrying poisonous spikes—for instance, small stingrays and rabbitfish—are often tortured to death before being thrown away or carried home for supper. Also adult men have been occasionally observed to molest poisonous and otherwise "bad" fish (fish with strong bites and sharp teeth, such as the moray eel and barracuda) before they are killed. In one instance an adult man furiously cut a stingray embryo to tiny pieces with his *parang* amid a crowd of children. When hunting with rubber-string harpoons, Miang Tuu boys and adult men rarely try to spear medium-sized stingrays and other fish that might inflict harm if clumsily handled. The meat of such fish is, however, regarded as a delicacy. When boys help out in netfishing they soon learn to watch out for the black poisonous sea urchin and the rabbitfish; the sting of the spikes of the sea urchin and various fish is quite painful and the pain may last for hours, even days.

Animals that fight are regarded as top entertainment by young and old in Miang Tuu. Cockfights staged for betting are illegal on Bonerate. However, two or three adult villagers and some boys in their early teens own pet cocks, which they feed well (poultry is generally not fed) and train for fights. Cock fights in Miang Tuu are held just to amuse the villagers and to train the birds. The fights are always interrupted before any harm is inflicted on any of the combatants. Both younger girls and boys stage minor fights with chickens and hens for entertainment. Children under the age of ten can often be observed carrying a chicken under one arm and holding a corncob in the hand. When they encounter a young cock, they put the chicken down and throw a grain between the two birds. The intention is, of course, to make the birds fight, which they usually do.

However, the more serious the fight is and the larger the fighting animals are, the greater the entertainment value. One day an incident in the village created enormous excitement. A band of boys and girls were running in triumph between the houses. A boy approximately eleven years old was in the lead. He threw a falcon high into the air. The bird flew and the village hens called out their frightened signals of danger. But both feet of the falcon were firmly tied to a length of strong fishing line. When the bird had flown out the total length of the line, it crash landed onto the ground. The children had spotted the falcon's nest some time ago and had just now managed to snare it. During the last weeks, falcons had killed two or three village chickens; today the roles were to be reversed. The hens should kill the predatory bird. First, the falcon was thrown to the various Miang Tuu cocks, which fiercely attacked their enemy. The falcon defended himself well, but his movements were restricted because of his inability to use his feet. When one cock was exhausted, the children grabbed the falcon and ran to the next cock, which was alerted by the noise and ready to fight. Slowly the village cocks pecked the energy and life out of the falcon. In the end the predator was thrown to a hen with eight young chickens trailing her. The hen was extremely fierce and did not give in before the falcon lay dead in front of her. During the "show" the children shouted and laughed excitedly. Adult villagers joined them to watch the fight, and they too got carried away with emotional shouts.

Once every year, horse fights are staged in Miang Tuu. Four horses, two mares and two stallions, are led into the village ground in mixed pairs. A forced "wife-swapping" is staged with the result that the stallions get furious and start to fight. The sight of the kicking and biting horses triggers tremendous excitement in the watching crowd of villagers. Children and adults alike scream and shout at the large, fighting animals. The fighting stallions may represent an unsolved and repressed oedipal conflict and may even be overdetermined by primary thought connotations related to male–female envy. Blessed with procreative abilities of mother-hood, the mares watch the stallions' virile fight to prove maleness and sexual responsibility. In addition, the horses' exhibition of their genitals is likely to connect to an unconscious lack of male self-respect in young boys due to dread of their own sexual inade-quacy vis-à-vis the mother. Anxiety may also be aroused in girls because of their own physiological immaturity and oedipal wishes (cf. Horney, 1973b, pp. 133–146).[8]

During these horse fights, Miang Tuu children have the unusual experience of observing their parents in strong and overt emo-tional behavior. Thus when the islanders are watching explicit aggressive behavior between animals, Bonerate culture, which so strictly prohibits much emotional display, provides an opportunity for relaxation from the generally operating norms of emotional restraint in a public context. The yearly horse fights are a great event in the life of the villagers. Children and adults are excited by the thought of the event's proximity, and they comment upon the fights long afterwards.

Finally, relations among children, dogs, and cats must be men-tioned briefly. Bonerate dogs are not kept as pets, but they are sup-posed to signal when strangers enter the village and to chase mon-keys away from the fields when the crops are maturing and ripening. Children, like adults, kick dogs, throw sticks at them when they get in the way or sometimes just for the fun of it. Dogs run away yelping every day because someone has kicked them.

Cats are treated inconsistently—sometimes patted and at other times kicked away. Young children find it amusing to play with cats. They may for instance dress them up in their *sarongs* or pet them. Girls and women seem to be more prone to pet cats than do older boys and men. When the cat gets tired of playing with the children and retreats, it is usually punished by kicks before it escapes. When food is prepared, cats are often given scraps, but when they try to help themselves to prepared dishes, they are kicked away. Children watch the cat and kick it just when the ani-mal opens its mouth for a good bite! Most households have at

---

[8] I have offered an interpretation of the social significance of this horse fight in a different context (Broch, 1985a).

least one cat. Once the cat of the household in which I lived disappeared for two weeks. When he returned, an enormous scar spread across the middle of his back. Somebody had slashed him with a *parang*. When my host commented on the incident, he explained that this was quite bad. "Cats are like children and should not be punished like that; you know a cat is not intentionally bad!"

Compared to Western children, Miang Tuu boys and girls appear to be obedient and nonviolent in most interactions. During my stay in the village, for instance, I did not observe a single occasion of dyadic fistfighting. Recurring temper tantrums, pouting, and sulking do, however, indicate that the children are not always on good terms with themselves and their social environment. Knowing this and remembering that hostility seems to be projected to objects outside the local community, we should not be surprised that some aggression is directed toward animals. In addition, the adult members of the society provide a legitimizing model for such behavior. I do, however, regard the expressed aggression as being of a somewhat different nature in the various cases, and they should accordingly be explained differently. Aggressive acts will often, of course, be overdetermined, and ideally we should account for both the latent and manifest sides of the phenomenon. In this discussion such a broad analysis is not possible; a tentative and partial examination will have to do.

What triggers the concrete aggressive acts is obviously related to the particular context. When the falcon is tortured or when poisonous fish are molested, a part of the aggressive rage is no doubt related to a feeling of hate toward that particular animal. The falcon is preying on chickens; the fish provokes pain when its poisonous spikes are touched. Aggression toward such animals may well be interpreted, at least on the manifest level, as an act of punishment and revenge. But that explanation does not tell us all; it does not account for the nature of the punishment. Likewise, it is difficult to understand why insects should be maimed before they are killed, or why they are killed at all after their service as play objects is ended.

When children play with ducks and chickens, which in various ways have to fight for delicious foods, the child may well identify with the animal. When fish is prepared for supper, children sometimes have temper tantrums because the particular species they like the best is given to or eaten by some other household member. This experience seems especially traumatic when the child has participated in fishing and has himself caught a particularly good fish that he is not given to eat. Later when the child is playing with birds, he can identify with the disappointed duck or the fighting chickens that are denied or have to fight for a delicacy. At the same time he gets revenge by being the determining master of the situation. The child is unaware that this is why he stages this play and finds it so amusing; his motivation here is grounded on preconscious thought processes. I have not said much about dogs in this context. Indeed, they are not loved. They are seldom fed and never let into the house, but the relationship between dogs and humans is still ambivalent.[9] The young child fears dogs. This is the repulsive animal that eats feces; perhaps early experiences when the dogs ate the child's warm excrement are still a disturbing memory. Chickens also eat excrement, but that fact, though observed by all villagers, has no cultural significance in Miang Tuu. The feeding habits of poultry do not make them repulsive. Neither are Bonerate cats particularly clean, but they are occasionally fed and allowed inside. Cats are beaten sometimes quite badly, but no one fears them. Of course, dogs are larger than cats and may bite much harder. But, to a child, the bite of a cat may be bad enough and the scratch of sharp claws can be painful and can cause infection. There are reasons enough to be afraid of cats, but these are not developed.

When dogs and cats are kicked by a child in a bad mood, this act is easily interpreted as displaced aggression. But sometimes these animals are kicked as soon as they are seen. The child seems to be acting on an impulse without a connecting link to any previous social situation. We should also remember how much children enjoy watching animals in aggressive encounters. Many psychological conflicts stem from the conflict of one's moral values with one's self-image, or from the violation of moral values by subconscious desires. Erikson holds that during the psychosocial development of children struggles of syntonic and dystonic ten-

---

[9] Through a brief period, Bonerate dogs were used for hunting the deer population of the island. Training dogs for hunting was an innovation in the community and in approximately two years' time this hunting resulted in lots of meat. But then the deer became extinct; the last animals were forced into the sea by packs of dogs hunting on their own. As mentioned, dogs are needed to guard fields and other property.

dencies—such as autonomy versus shame and doubt, and initiative versus guilt—are particularly forceful (Erikson, 1982, pp. 55–61). These and other inner conflicts are

> tension producing and painful and thus motivate the individual to in some way seek to reduce tension. Defence mechanisms, such as repression, sublimation and displacement are techniques which protect the individual from the pain born of psychological conflict. (Singer, 1978, p. 272)

It is through a type of culturally constituted displacement of aggression that the Miang Tuu children's behavior toward animals can best be understood. Because of the cultural importance placed on nonviolent and nonaggressive cooperation within this small community, the Miang Tuuans have developed means to ban internal, intercommunity aggression. As we have seen, this ideology is firmly manifested in the socialization of children. But when tensions do occur and accumulate in young as well as in adults, aggression is displaced in a culturally approved way onto objects such as various animals. What is observed among the Ifaluk, that "instead of permitting hostility to be expressed in social relations, . . . culture directed its expression into other, less, disruptive channels" (Spiro, 1980, p. 343), is equally true in Miang Tuu.

It should also be plausible that children, as well as adults, may identify with fighting animals. Watching the fights may at least in some instances offer another release for accumulated inner tensions. To put it somewhat differently, children torture animals and enjoy watching animal aggression; both activities are exciting and good entertainment. In addition to the dramatic and entertaining aspect, the motivation for the emotional involvement of the children is to be looked for in the unconscious, rooted in the constitution of self and the cultural predicaments acquired through processes of socialization. How displacement of aggression is designed to serve as a psychological defense mechanism is difficult to test or verify on the interactional level, or through open or structured interviews with children. However, the psychological constitution and behavior of the adult population is relevant to the interpretation of child behavior. This is particularly true in the Miang Tuu context, where the parents and older generations provide a quite consistent model of behavior to the children of the village. Also because we can turn this argument around and claim that Miang Tuu parents and other major caretakers of children themselves had a very similar socialization to the one children experience today, we must be able to assume that there is a high degree of repetition in the range of social, cultural, and psychological constitution in the individuals growing up in Miang Tuu. The child's values and the norms guiding his behavior are constituted not only on the model of his parents, but also on the idiosyncratic and cultural ideals of the same parents.

Owati and Yobaida

Like Leipi and Halimu, Owati and Yobaida were best friends. The two girls, approximately eleven and nine years old, spent much of their time together, but their interaction was colored by their different social status. The options for their adaption to daily life within the village were different and made the cultural emphasis on social position quite explicit. Owati, the daughter of *bapak* and *ibu lingkung,* could be regarded the most fortunate of the two. On the most tangible level, Owati's luck could be measured by all her dresses and *sarongs.* Yobaida sometimes borrowed a dress from Owati, but usually she wore a faded *sarong.* But more importantly, Owati was able to delegate some chores she did not like to do herself to her friends, for instance to Yobaida. The consequence was not that Owati gained much more leisure than other village girls. She tended her niece until Yobaida was given that responsibility. However, it was suspected that Owati would take on the task and responsibility of tending another baby who was soon to be born. As we shall se, Owati did quite a number of things other girls usually did not engage in. This may have been the result of a sense of sex-role frustration that most other village girls did not experience. Owati did not have to help in the house if she did not want to do so, and she showed signs of frustration when she was prohibited from participating in male activities such as fishing. She was an excellent swimmer and, unlike most other girls her age, she showed great endurance in diving.

Owati loved her father very much, and he returned her love by affective means such as bringing her goodies. But when the girl wanted to imitate her father in various ways, she was sometimes frustrated because he could not grant her wishes. His frustration was exposed when he explained his concerns for his daughter to the anthropologist. Owati was the oldest girl in the village who frequently had severe temper tantrums. The frustration that triggered these moods was always the same. She either became jealous of her younger brother or angry with her father when he refused to take her along to fish. I neither observed nor heard about other girls' wanting to do the things that Owati wanted so badly. Owati did not want to fish in the usual manner of Bonerate women, with a bamboo pole, hook, and line; she wanted to dive or fish from a dugout canoe far out on the ocean. We have seen that Bonerate gender roles often overlap, but when Owati wanted to accompany her father, she picked the most explicitly male activities available.

Like Owati, Yobaida had a younger brother. Although he was closer to her in age than Owati's brother was to her, I never observed Yobaida express jealousy of her brother by having tantrums. As far as I could see, Yobaida always obeyed and did whatever she was told to do by her mother or by members of the *ibu lingkung* household, where she served during the last months of my stay in the village. Yobaida's father was at sea and away from the island most of the year. Yobaida lived with her mother and siblings in a house of average quality. Her mother was a hard-working woman who looked after their own field when her husband was away. She occasionally worked some hours and even whole days for *ibu lingkung,* doing such jobs as harvesting cassava. She also agreed that Yobaida would serve on various occasions in the household of *ibu lingkung.* Measured by Miang Tuu standards, Yobaida was not from a poor family; rather, hers represented an economically viable household.

Both Owati and Yobaida were circumcised before I arrived on Bonerate.

The description of Owati will be emphasized here, as she represents an exception in several ways within the village context. Yobaida emerges as contrast to Owati's behavior and, as soon will become clear, she passively complements her friend's role. Yobaida's situation is similar to that of most girls her age in Miang Tuu.

"Look at her, that girl is not afraid," *kepala lingkung* tells me. Riding on his horse with his youngest son on the same animal in front of him, he has just returned from *ibu kota.* Owati sits on her horse as on a throne. It is clear to everyone that she loves horseback riding. She receives many admiring glances from the villagers. They say that of course women may ride, but they usually do not want to because they are afraid. Owati's three older sisters say that they do not like to ride and have never wanted to do so. One of them tried once, but she was thrown off and never tried again. Owati was also thrown off once, I am told, but she got angry and demanded to be placed back on the horse at once! Even Owati's father has fallen off his horse and has a large scar on his cheek where the animal kicked him. Although everyone agrees that it is quite proper for women to ride, no Miang Tuu women do and only one girl, Owati, does.

If we follow Anna Freud, Owati's horse-craze could indicate penis envy, as shown in her powerful handling of the animal as an extension of her body; or phallic sublimation as expressed in her ambition to master the horse and to perform on it (cf. Freud, 1965, p. 20). Owati never showed any interest in grooming, feeding, or looking after the horse. Owati was in no way obsessed by the horse or her own horsemanship. She enjoyed riding and excelling on horseback, but she never rode for leisure. Her riding was always within a particular context, such as going to *ibu kota* with her father to sell fish.

When Owati went on a voyage with her parents to Java, the Miang Tuuans agreed that the village became remarkably quiet. At her return, play activities almost exploded with Owati's initiatives! As described in Chapter 2, that homecoming of Owati was a painful experience to Yobaida, who had been in charge of baby Kartini during her friend's absence. Owati took Kartini away from Yobaida when it pleased her, and she returned "Tini" to the attention of her friend when the baby became a drag! Thus, Yobaida and Kartini were dependent on the will and moods of Owati in the development of their dyadic relationship.

At about the same time, Yobaida moved into the household of *ibu lingkung* and spent a period there helping with various tasks, such as fetching water, sweeping the floors, and laying the "table." In fact, she took over many chores Owati had been doing. Now Owati was free to engage in other activities, such as assisting her sisters with food preparations and making coconut oil. She also soon became remarkably prone to delegate to Yobaida the tasks she previously seemed to enjoy. She may have discovered that her position allowed her to have her work done by her friends. And this arrangement did not noticeably alter the friendly relationship between Yobaida and Owati. They continued to play together, remained best friends, and shared each others' company more than that of any other girls. Yobaida also continued to be devoted to Owati; the two were never observed to quarrel or fight.

One activity Owati enjoyed was touring the village to sell various items, such as *tape* or fish, that she carried on her head. Now she brought Yobaida along to carry the goods for sale on her head, while she herself handled the money and discussions of quality and price. The arrangement was innovative in Miang Tuu. Nobody remembered having seen such a division of tasks before and definitely not among children. Nor did adult villagers behave in this way. When, however, some traders arrived from distant islands with *sarongs* for sale, it happened that the "boss" brought along assistants to display the material but not to handle the transactions.

When *bapak lingkung* and I returned at dawn from a night's fishing, we were met by Owati and Yobaida on the beach. The two girls inspected the catch. Owati sent her friend home to get a basket for the fish. Owati remained with us and asked her father for permission to join us next time we went fishing. He did not answer her. When Yobaida returned, Owati loaded the basket with fish and placed it on Yobaida's head. Fishy water dripped down on Yobaida's hair and body while the two girls walked across the village. Owati carried only a shark by its tail, its head dragged along in the dust.

A couple of weeks earlier the two girls had both eagerly carried the catch home, but now Owati took on the role of her mother. Before, when we returned from fishing, it was *ibu* who came down to view the catch. It was *ibu* who organized the bringing home of the fish. Now Yobaida returned a second time to the beach to get the remaining fish while Owati stayed at the house. Only Yobaida had to take a bath after the job was done! When she had washed herself, she was given some fish to take home to her mother although Yobaida herself would eat with Owati.

Of all the jobs Yobaida was asked to do, there was one that I believe she really did not like. Sometimes when *bapak lingkung* wanted to rest, for instance after a fishing expedition, he summoned Yobaida to groom his hair and kill any lice she could find. Lying in the bed, *bapak* found the grooming pleasant. He closed his eyes. The little girl soon grew tired with boredom. She seemed to want to get away to join her playmates outside. Her movements became slower while she peeped out between the wall boards. *Bapak* cleared his throat, and Yobaida started afresh. She looked at the children of the house who passed by, but they were not summoned, and none wanted to take on her job. When the little girl was finally through, she walked to the kitchen and was given something to eat before she joined the other children in play.

Once or twice I observed Owati and Leipi groom their father's hair, but they did not continue for long. They stopped when they felt like it, and they were not asked to continue. Their act was one of emotional concern, while Yobaida had to do a job.

Earlier in this chapter I pointed to the explicit expression of social inequality in the relationship of Leipi and Halimu. The same arguments have relevance here, but instead of repeating what has already been said, I shall here dwell on one aspect of the psychosocial development of Owati. I have claimed that she seemed to be less secure in her gender role than most other girls her age. I argued that this impression was based on her identification with her father, her love for him, and her striving for a partial masculine role play. But a change occurred in Owati's behavior during my stay. What did not change was her repeated expressions of being someone unique, different from the rest of the children her age, and perhaps different from most other villagers. Before her trip to Java, she expressed herself through tantrums of frustration over not being allowed to be close to her father whenever she wanted. Perhaps she also envied her brother because, as a boy, he was allowed to be with their father when she was not. She did not point her rage directly toward her mother or father. The tantrums expressed mere frustration over a rather complex situation. Although her conflict was surely overdetermined, I have here pointed only at some rather explicit dimensions of that conflict.

After the return from Java, I did not observe Owati going through such temper tantrums again. She also appeared less demanding in her relationship with her father. She would make an attempt to share his company at fishing, but she did not demand an answer as before. I believe that during the voyage, which lasted for more than a month, Owati outgrew some of her gender frustration. On her return to the island, she had found a new way to cope with her internal wishes of being in control, and she had found a new dimension within which she could define her relationship with her father. Now she was able to get narcissistic gratification by applying the culturally accepted norms of gender performance. Bonerate women are, as mentioned, great administrators of many tasks. Given Owati's social position within the village, she took advantage of the options her own sex granted her. Her behavior after her return was clearly modeled on her mother. She was copying her own mother in a slightly exaggerated manner. But let me finally turn to Owati on the horse. In that context she did not imitate her mother but added an individual dimension to her role performance. *Ibu* would never ride a horse. Owati expanded her script to include being the master of horses. To Bonerate islanders that animal symbolizes danger, wildness, virility, strength, and power—all of which the girl symbolically controlled. That the villagers share this interpretation of symbolic force was demonstrated when Owati was allowed to carry on her signal activity as the girl who was in charge. But given the social context of Bonerate, horses also signify and perhaps also symbolize the social position of their masters. Only individuals of relative wealth or high social status own horses, and Owati utilizes this idea to her personal advantage, to confirm her psychosocial status.

The same options were not open to Yobaida. First, she did not show the same signs of frustration as her friend. Yobaida never revolted from her role by tantrums; rather, she passively accepted fate. Given the social position of her family, which she did not protest, her behavior was at least socially adaptive. This, however, tells us little of her psychological constitution of gratifications and potential inner conflicts. Second, it is possible that the differences in socialization between the children of the more affluent *ibu* and *bapak lingkung* and the rest of the villagers provide a setting in which the children of the latter become more dependent than the former. The material presented here on socialization processes in the village points in that direction. I am speculating that the psychological consequences of the somewhat greater autonomy awarded the children of *ibu* and *bapak lingkung* may lead them to expect that they will play the role of initiators and leaders. On the other hand, the majority of the villagers tend to relate their social position to a large degree to a fate they cannot change but must cope with. The child's identification with his or her parents and their social position is difficult to change, because it is the product of a profound inference that is continually supported by evidence that strengthens the original belief (see Kagan, 1977). And in this context the closed nature of Miang Tuu society must again be stressed. Very few impulses that could give rise to ideas about social mobility within the community penetrate the village from outside.

CHAPTER 4

Late Childhood and Early Puberty

Circumcision Ceremonies

Bonerate girls and boys are all circumcised. Since the early 1970s circumcision of boys has, however, gradually ceased to be carried out in Miang Tuu. The operation is now usually done in a hospital in Surabaya, Java, during the boys' first trip to sea as members of a *perahu* crew at the ages of from fourteen to seventeen years. Consequently, no ceremonies or rituals are conducted, and boys are older than they used to be when circumcised.

For Miang Tuu villagers, this development has brought both relief and approval. Especially fathers told how they feared the circumcision of their sons in earlier days as there was so much pain and, worse, the practice involved a very real risk of death for the novices. Boys who were uncircumcised said they too were happy the operation now could be done at a hospital because those who had that experience could tell them that there was really nothing to it.[1] As far as I could detect, the abolition of male circumcision rituals from the village scene had not seriously altered male status. The villagers apparently did not treat young men circumcised at a hospital differently from those who had undergone circumcision ceremonies on Bonerate. This attitude differs from that in many

---

[1] In some few instances, Bonerate boys are circumcised on the island by barefoot doctors. A feast is arranged afterwards to which all villagers are invited. This happens when it becomes clear that a boy will not go to sea or it is unlikely he will leave the island and have the operation in a hospital.

other societies where traditional rituals have changed or disappeared. From the African Gisu it is reported that

> Gisu are convinced that it is the progress of initiates through the initiation rituals which makes circumcision a validation of male authority, not merely the physical change. A youth circumcised in a hospital is not thereby made a man for he has not withstood the ordeal. (La Fontaine, 1977, p. 425)

Various cultures provide their men with different means to achieve and display masculinity. Circumcision rituals surely were one way of gaining male identity at Bonerate, but so also was piracy another arena, now lost, for achieving and proving masculinity. The mere act of *perahu* sailing, an arduous activity, is cognitively regarded as a supermasculine undertaking. Thus the first trip to sea as a fresh crew member might serve as a more tangible initiation ritual, marking a transition from child to adult, than the circumcision rituals alone.

As I interpret Bonerate circumcision rituals, they are not unquestionable initiation rituals whose major function is to mark a change from child to adult status. But to this I shall return later in this chapter. First I shall outline male circumcision as it was practiced only a few years ago, and then I will examine Bonerate female circumcision rituals as they exist in Miang Tuu today.

Male Circumcision

Male informants always remembered the pain they had gone through in circumcision, stressing their fright first as novices and later as fathers of novices. No educational value of the ritual was mentioned beyond the Koranic readings in Arabic, a language they did not understand. Usually circumcision was arranged for three or four boys at the same time. Their age would range from six to fifteen years. Parents of boys who were not yet circumcised got together and decided who should be circumcised and when; then the boys and all villagers were told. There were extensive preparations; food for a feast had to be provided and uniforms rented from *ibu kota,* Bonerate. The morning of the day the ritual performances started the boys' fingernails were painted red. The boys were dressed in knee-long *sarong*s and their naked waists were adorned with gold and silver coins—English, Dutch, all kinds! On their heads were sharp-pointed admiral hats. That was the traditional costume on Bonerate, I was told.[2]

The novices were gathered and an older man read from the Koran. Somewhat later the same day, the operation was done with a bamboo knife, which the informants said sometimes was not as sharp as it should have been! Because they could not stand to see the pain of their children, two fathers told me that they had fled to the woods when their sons were circumcised. After the prepuce had been severed, powder made from dried coconut-palm leaves was applied to the wound to prevent infection. The prepuce was wrapped in a piece of white cloth and tied to the top branches of a large tree. This was done in order to achieve a future wife of high social standing (white cloth was formerly a standard part of Bonerate and Miang Tuu bridewealth). To prevent competition among the novices, only one prepuce was attached to each tree.

Pain and blood are attached to circumcision for boys. This is repeated over and over again by men to emphasize the important contrast to female circumcision, which at Bonerate does not provoke pain and blood. Boys were in severe pain for at least a week, usually longer. Every morning they would be carried down to the beach to sit in the ocean water because that would reduce the pain and prevent infections. When I asked if death ever resulted from infections in connection with circumcision, I unintentionally initiated the only heated discussion I heard in Miang Tuu. I was talking to five men, two of whom immediately confirmed that death sometimes had occurred. The others became quite upset about that answer. They said circumcision had never caused the death of a novice; that death (in these instances) was due to quite different reasons. They did agree, however, that circumcision had been a painful experience they would never forget. The boys who were circumcised were all well looked after. They were supported to the beach and helped home again. They got good food, and it was regarded as important for them to sleep a lot. At night villagers

---

[2] On this point there is some confusion. Commoners on the island were severely punished if they wore the colors or costumes of the nobility. What is here referred to as traditional dress resembles the clothing of nobles. Either the informants wanted to impress me, or they referred to the most recent rituals when the rules for dressing were weakening. Today everyone dresses as they wish or can afford.

would come to their homes to talk. When they were feeling better the boys would be sent for by different neighbors and served tea, coffee, and cakes; this was indeed special treatment because, even for parties, tea and coffee are too expensive. It was a good feeling to be in the center of village attention, as one of the informants remarked. Many times people would gather and play the *gambus,* or they would sing songs to make the boys forget their pain.[3]

Female Circumcision

Girls are usually "circumcised" some years earlier than boys, that is, at from six to twelve years or an approximate average of eight years. Circumcision may be held for one or more girls at a time. Women say that girls who go through the rituals together normally develop close friendships that last throughout life. As for the boys, circumcisions of girls are public village events; however, initiations of girls and boys are never held at the same time. Arranging the ceremonies is expensive. This is another factor that affects the parents' decision about when their daughters should be circumcised. Food has to be provided. The rituals last for two days, during which all villagers are fed three times. Special costumes are rented, and a ritual leader is hired. She usually has a good reputation for various skills such as curing diseases and being a good midwife. If convenient and possible, she will often be the same woman who received the novice at birth.

I shall in some detail describe the circumcision ritual arranged for Jamilan, a Miang Tuu girl, while I was in the village. Jamilan, approximately twelve years old, was living alone with her mother in a two-room house. Her father was dead, but a maternal uncle and his wife helped with the preparations and made large contributions. As usual when a feast is prepared, a *gotong royong* (cooperative work) was arranged to make the food.

For some time all Miang Tuu villagers have known that Jamilan would soon be circumcised. Her relatives who live in other Bonerate villages have also been notified.

The morning the ritual starts, the house of Jamilan's mother is decorated under the supervision of the ritual expert, a middle-aged

---

[3] No one owned a *gambus* or any other instrument in condition to be played during my stay in the village.

woman who has her house in the *ibu kota*. Half an hour or so after sunset, guests arrive at the home of the novice. They are women and men, young and old, relatives and special friends of the novice, and people of high social standing.

At the right side of the entrance, a large coconut flower cluster is nailed to the outside wall. Inside the room two Petromax oil lanterns are giving off a bright, cool light. The room is cleared except for one large bed, which is placed in the interior left corner. The bed is supplied with lots of *bundels* (sausage-shaped pillows) and dressed in white sheets. Jamilan is sitting cross-legged at the head of the bed; she is dressed in a bright-colored *sarong* and a blouse. She wears shining bracelets on her arms and several golden coins around her neck. Beside her on the bed, five eggs are placed on a tiny tray. The ritual expert is seated on a chair close to Jamilan in the bed. Now and then she talks to the girl or smooths her dress, which she brought along this morning. Several of Jamilan's playmates who are not yet circumcised are also present. They stand around the bed with admiring expressions on their faces; sometimes they whisper to the novice.

A boy in his teens, not yet circumcised, sits by the foot end of the bed. He is given a small stone pestle and with slow regular movements he grinds some leaves (possibly henna). Some water is added to form a mush called *batiranga*. The ritual expert uses this to paint all of Jamilan's fingernails. When the *batiranga* is dry, the nails have a bright, dark, red color. After this is done, the ritual expert retires. The small girls present get a little braver and are allowed to touch Jamilan's jewelry. Now and then some older girls, not married but circumcised, keep Jamilan company for a while and talk quietly to her.

When the guests arrive, they discreetly hand the novice a small sum of money. Jamilan is playing with it while she sits in the bed. After a while she climbs out of the bed and slips behind the cloth wall that separates the two rooms of the house. The ritual expert reappears, smooths the sheets, removes the eggs, and follows Jamilan.

The guests remain seated on the floor. Men and women are sitting in separate groups, but talking together. Food is served, the usual coarse-grained corn and some cucumbers boiled in water. Young village girls help with the serving. After the meal, locally grown tobacco is offered, and most men help themselves and make their own cigarettes. Four men play dominos; the rest of the guests keep on chatting for a while. It is soon late at night in Miang Tuu; by ten o'clock all guests return to their homes.

The next morning at half past seven the feast goes on. A communal village meal is served. Because of limited space three separate servings are organized. Close relatives and those with the highest social status are fed first. The food offered is rice, tiny pieces of fish meat, and cucumbers boiled in water. After the food, lukewarm water is served and tobacco brought forth. Jamilan is not to be seen during the meal.

After all villagers are served, the day wears on, taking on the character of a "holiday."[4] All men relax, but most women and young girls are busy taking turns preparing food for the large communal meal to be held in the evening. Some are cooking at large fires at different locations in the village, others at their home fireplaces. Hens are plucked and fish cured (hens are eaten only on special occasions).

Nobody seems to know when the circumcision will take place, but everybody remains in the village. People walk around or sit down and talk. At noon the women bring some food to their homes from the common kitchens and feed their families.

Finally, in the late afternoon Jamilan appears. Accompanied by her mother and the ritual expert, she crosses the village to her father's brother's house. It is here the "circumcision" will take place. Soon all villagers know that the novice has left her home, and little by little, most of them gather outside the house. I am told that when girls are circumcised there is no blood, no wound, no pain, and no health risk involved. The circumcision is a symbolic act that consists of a light scratch with a bamboo knife at the inside of the upper thigh. I asked girls who had been circumcised not too long ago about this, but the only answer they volunteered with a smile was that yes, there is no pain.

After circumcision Jamilan's body is covered with a mixture of rice and corn flour that is blended with pleasant-smelling herbs.[5] Her eyebrows are painted with golden corn flour. I was given no

---

[4] Holidays are rare in Miang Tuu. Work is carried on all days of the week. During the year I lived on Bonerate, only three or four days went by without normal work being done by the members of the household in which I lived.

[5] Women often apply this mixture to themselves and young children to cool their bodies and to protect their skin from the sun.

explanation as to why that was done. After Jamilan's body is treated in this way, she is once more dressed in the costume brought by the ritual expert. This time her hair is also covered with a transparent lilac shawl. When dressed, the "circumcised" girl needs to rest before she can return to her home. But she is ready and permitted to give audience to visitors. All the small girls in Miang Tuu enter the house to admire her beauty. Both men and women pay short visits and give her gifts of money (Rp. 10 to 100).

More and more people gather outside the house. Some have been waiting almost two hours for Jamilan to come out. Both women and men are present. Some men entertain the crowd by imitating war dances using wooden sticks instead of swords. Finally all the small girls flow out, and everybody outside stands up; they try to get close to the ladder to get a good view. And now Jamilan appears in the door opening. Everybody cheers or whistles. She walks slowly down the wooden ladder alone. Jamilan seems tiny, pale, and exhausted. She is *malu* (shy) and looks bothered and a little frightened. The body paint and the vivid colors of her costume make her complexion look even paler. At the bottom of the ladder, two men are ready to carry her. With their hands they make a seat for her. She puts one arm around the neck of each of them and is lifted up from the last step of the ladder to a position where she is sitting between them. At this moment the ritual expert appears. She throws rice that pours down on Jamilan. An adolescent boy shades her head from the sun with an umbrella while she is carried rapidly home. Young children are trailing the procession, shouting and cheering loudly as they run. Adults are following at a slower pace. When Jamilan is carried up the ladder into her mother's house, more rice is thrown. A man standing close to me says, "They should not throw rice; that was what people did in the old days." He means it is a heathen custom. After a while Jamilan's maternal uncle appears at the door; he is calling for attention. The first serving is due. People have already been told which serving they are to share. The first is reserved for the village elder, guests from other villages, and others of high social standing.

Inside, Jamilan is again present, sitting on the bed. Now all the white sheets that were decorating it last night have been removed. She is all alone, the colored eggs at her side. The guests seem to ignore her. Jamilan keeps her eyes down and seems not to know what to look at. The room is crowded with people looking forward to a meal. Jamilan first idly fingers a corner of her *sarong,* then does the same to her blouse; she turns the bracelet on one of her wrists, round and round. Slowly she changes her cross-legged position just a little, stretches out one leg, then sits quietly again. She starts to play with money given to her, gets hold of a coin and turns it round and round and round. Not once, not even a brief moment am I able to observe her sight fixed on somebody or anything outside the bed on which she is sitting.

The guests are seated on the floor. Women and men, about equal numbers of each sex, are separated into distinct groups. But the room is so crowded that the backs of many men and women touch. The men sit closest to the entrance, the women at the back of the room near the kitchen area. Jamilan's mother walks about and greets all her guests by a handshake. She begins with the oldest man in the village. In front of him is a big pillow on which five large plates filled with rice are placed. On the top of the convex-shaped rice on each plate rests a fried egg. The old man reads from the Koran in Arabic and thus blesses the food. Two of the blessed plates are handed to the women; the other three are given to the men. The eating starts. The guests eat fast and silently; rice, pieces of chicken, cold fish, and noodles are served. As the guests one by one are satisfied, they give a sign and a glass of lukewarm water is passed to them. The glass is half emptied, refilled, and handed to the next. The feast has come to an end, and the guests leave the room; some walk home, others squat outside to chat and smoke. The next serving is ready. When the third serving is completed and all guests have come out, some small girls enter the house to keep Jamilan company. She has been sitting on the bed all the time and has not received any food. Now she can relax.

The next morning Jamilan was once again outdoors playing with the other children, just as she used to before the circumcision ritual took place. I was not able to observe any significant change in her pattern of behavior that day or in the days that followed.

After the ritual I wanted to find out why Jamilan looked so pale and worn when she reappeared from her paternal uncle's house. Few, if any, seemed to have noticed that she appeared extraordinarily pale after circumcision. But if, indeed, I were right, the informants agreed it had to be due to the heat. She had to sit very quietly for a long time listening to the ritual expert. And, further Jamilan had to be very careful, especially when walking down the ladder. Any quick movements would cause the dress to tear. That dress was very old and easily torn. That had to be why she looked tired.[6]

A Closer Look at Circumcision Rituals

The data presented on male and female circumcision differ in kind and also in the amount of cultural information. In spite of these and other shortcomings, we can compare the rituals for similarities and major differences.

Usually circumcision rituals are regarded as initiation rituals whose social function is

> to help ensure a smooth transition from childhood to adulthood in those societies where either individual personality or social structural factors are likely to interfere with a smooth transition. (Levinson & Malone, 1980, p. 215)

Initiation rituals are generally divided for descriptive and analytic purposes into three stages: separation, transition, and incorporation. During the separation, the novices are removed from the daily setting of their natal home, both in space and symbolically. During the transition stage, the status of the novices is often ambivalent. At this time physical ordeals, teaching of discipline, or circumcision may take place. This may often be a period of rather formalized education, even in societies that lack institutionalized education in other contexts. When this transitional stage is completed, the novices return to the village or home where they gain public recognition of their newly achieved status. Thus in many cultures the initiates come to the separation stage as children, but by the time of their reunion with relatives, they are grown adults. This is, as we have seen above, not the case in Miang Tuu. I have already suggested that circumcision on Bonerate is not an initiation ritual that transforms children into adults. Rather, initiation here inaugurates the children to a culturally accepted notion of a period of gradual development that leads toward adult life and status. During the circumcision rituals, the

---

[6] Bonerate islanders equate a pale or light complexion with beauty.

novices are taught aspects of ideal Bonerate conduct that they will
need to know when they mature both physically and mentally. But
the circumcision rituals also serve several other ends. For instance,
the initiates themselves serve as symbols for the Miang Tuu villagers by their display of idealized social norms. Thus, as a reminder,
the event is equally important to young and old alike. Like most
rituals, circumcision ceremonies have multiple symbolic meanings
and functions.

If we consider the similarities and parallels of male and female
circumcision, we find that the rituals share several elements commonly found in most initiation rituals regardless of culture. Thus
it is older, more experienced persons, renowned for their ritual
skills, who are in charge of the ceremonies. These ritual leaders
also play the role of formal educators of social norms and standards in everyday behavior and religious respect. To emphasize
the uniqueness of the event, the novices are dressed in special out-
fits not to be worn under other circumstances. Also the parading
in the appropriate uniforms provides the initiates with the villagers' approval, which may strengthen the sex identity and self-
image of the novices. They are the princesses[7] or princes of
the day.

The parents of the novices are peripheral in much of the ritual
but play an important role in the more profane parts of the ceremonies. The mother and the father of the novice contribute by
providing foods for the feast.

The ritual expert is of the same sex as the initiates. Further, permission to be present at the crucial act of circumcision is restricted
to a few who are of the same sex as the novice. The rituals underline an interconnected unity between the initiates and the community of which they are a part. The villagers provide the setting:
they offer both material support in the form of money and labor,
and moral support by their very presence, their cheering, and their
nurturance of the newly circumcised. The initiates symbolize the
viable community by a focus on reproductivity; they demonstrate
rules of conduct, sex roles, and social positions, and they also
serve as village integrators.

Circumcision in Miang Tuu is done to all boys and girls in the

---

[7] The umbrella and the yellow color (corn flour) are both symbols of royalty common in
Southeast Asia (Dentan, 1978: 101).

village. The rituals are focused on the initiates, both as a group and as individuals. In a small village such as Miang Tuu, a child who soon will or already has entered puberty does not have to wait for circumcision until a suitable number of other children of the same sex are ready to be initiated. Circumcision can be carried out for a single child, as in the case of Jamilan, although that is not thought to be the ideal way. A single initiant does not have the comfort of experiencing the ritual in company with peers. Thus he or she will not be able to develop the special friendship that usually develops among novices who are initiated at the same time. Also the expenses of the parents of initiates for the necessary preparations are reduced in proportion to the number of initiants, unless some novices are siblings.

In addition to these fairly universal traits in Miang Tuu circumcision rituals, there are other elements that are more locally colored. The information, particularly that on male initiation, is poor, so there might well be more ritual parallels than those presented here. Miang Tuu circumcision rituals are syncretistic in the sense that both Islamic and traditional elements are blended. During the ceremonies, paragraphs are read from the Koran in Arabic (as is done in other contexts in which food is distributed at feasts). It is important that the connections to Islam are emphasized in this way during circumcision, because the ritual sets the rule for proper behavior in the village. It is not what the text says that is important, because nobody understands Arabic. It is the fact that it is read, that a particular sacred relation is established, that is important.

The novices have to control their emotional expression at least during the public parts of the ritual. Because of the way this theme is elaborated, it should be emphasized in our discussion. Being able to control one's emotions, as pointed out in earlier chapters, is related to the cognitive model Miang Tuu villagers use to separate children from adults. Children are not responsible for most violations of social rules and norms, and they are not thought able to control their emotions. Adults are by definition capable of not getting carried away by emotional display. Neither newly circumcised boys nor girls are supposed to be capable of presenting a new self-image in everyday village encounters right away. That takes time, and adulthood is finally reached after marriage and the birth of the first child. But during circumcision rituals the novices are formally introduced to the ideal standards of conduct to which adults should conform. In this context the concept of being *malu* is highly significant. An aspect of *malu* behavior involves shame and respect for others in interaction. Individuals therefore must know their social position. After circumcision boys and girls are supposed to gradually pay more attention to these matters. The ritual not only presents the ideal answers on how to behave in interpersonal relations, but also offers clues about how to feel about one's actions. What Hildred Geertz wrote about the Javanese in this matter is just as relevant in Miang Tuu: "the important thing is not the sincerity of the action, but the successful cover up of all dissonant elements in the relationship" (Geertz, 1974, p. 257).

After circumcision, neither girls nor boys are allowed to show their genitals in public. This means that modesty has to be shown from now on. Girls always wear a *sarong* when washing themselves at the village wells or when they take a bath in the ocean. Boys have to show similar modesty. However, children are usually adjusted to this behavior before the day of their circumcision. Another component of adult behavior, which gradually becomes more and more relevant from this point on, is a role distance in the interaction between the father and his children, especially his sons. Also the context of task assignments to the initiated girl and boy involve new dimensions. They are now given more assignments and after a while are supposed to contribute more to the needs of their households. The actual tasks may not differ from those they previously were involved with. It is not the task performed that is crucial to one's status but the context of the task situation.

During the first stage of the rituals, the fingernails of both girls and boys are painted red. The same is also done to bride and groom at the time of their wedding. Miang Tuu villagers offered no explanation for this except that this is how it always has been done. According to Bugis traditions, however, the red color will shine like embers in the ultimate darkness. In other words, if the initiates should die, their souls would be guided to the other side of the dark by the red light (Paeni, personal communication, 1979).[8]

---

[8] I have no reason to believe that the implications would be different on Bonerate. The informants may have thought this belief to be in contradiction to Islam and therefore were reluctant to explain it. Perhaps they did not know or simply had forgotten.

With the exception of the painting of the fingernails, most of the other parallels found in the circumcision rituals of both boys and girls can be regarded as expressing gender-neutral adult conduct. If that is correct, it should follow that most of the differences and particularities in the two rituals would symbolize sex and sex-role-related issues. We can also assume that the elements most elaborated in rituals and in the memory of those who have passed through them point toward culturally crucial issues.

In the way men described their own and their sons' circumcision rituals, one thing is striking: they talk about the event in what might be interpreted as female metaphors. They might have been describing menstruation or the birth of children. Because fathers could not stand to watch the pain, they left the scene both at the time of the birth of their children and at the time of their sons' circumcision. It seems reasonable that these fathers withdrew because they feared they would not be able to control their emotions. By Bonerate standards, it would be extremely out of place not to be able to control one's emotions either at the moment your son is taught adult behavior (that is, emotional control) or at the moment your own adult status is finally and publicly confirmed, (that is, at the time of the birth of your first child). As we remember, this restraint is not required of women. To give birth is regarded as painful, and the mother has no restrictions on her expression of that pain.

In the minds of men who have experienced the circumcision ritual, two memories overshadow everything else: pain and blood. These two elements are also very much in the center of the female mysteries of menstruation and giving birth. Just as giving birth implies a health risk for the mother, male circumcision implies a health risk for the novice. Bettelheim has elaborated on the necessity of keeping male initiation secret and has drawn attention to circumcision as a symbol of male menstruation, an envy of women's procreativity (Bettelheim, 1962). I have also suggested elsewhere that in Bonerate culture can be found traits of a male envy of the female reproduction capacity (Broch, 1983). The fact that it seems so important to men to emphasize the difference between male and female circumcision, specifically with regard to pain and blood, may give further support to the notion of male–female envy on Bonerate. The pain men experience does not place them ahead of women, but it makes them more equal. Then, the abolition of male circumcision in Miang Tuu, if other major cultural changes do not follow, should not necessarily lead to role confusion among men or to a reduced male status, but rather to a growing male–female envy!

The importance of wrapping the prepuce in white cloth before placing it in a treetop expresses another endemic Bonerate male dilemma. Women do not lose status by marrying down, but men do. On the other hand, the most unfortunate of all marriages are those in which the man is not able to equal his wife and parents-in-law (Broch, 1983). Thus if you climb too high, the branches of the tree will break and you will fall down.

Male circumcision is thus not so much about sex roles as about helping the adult man overcome or resolve his inherent psychological dilemmas. The ritual elements stressing ideal male behavior in the everyday village context may have been forgotten or discounted by my informants. The admiral's hat is, however, an indication of anticipated male status and role behavior. This hat may well refer to the only positions a woman Bonerate islander can never achieve or come close to, that of a *juragan* (*perahu* captain) and his crew (Broch, 1983, 1985a). The hat may also refer to piracy. I was told that, as pirates, fathers of present villagers dressed in colorful costumes with bandoliers and hats. But the natural connection to seamanship brings us to the suggestion that male sex roles and male self-consciousness were to a large degree achieved at sea. Men, not children, return from sea.[9]

Several authors have pointed out that circumcision of boys occurs in societies where an emotionally close relationship is fostered between mother and son (Whiting, Kluckhon, & Anthony, 1958; Honigman, 1967; Brown, 1963). Bonerate boys, as we have seen, share the bed of their mothers during infancy. They are for long periods reared by their mothers when the fathers are at sea. Although this impact is somewhat moderated by the child care of grandfathers, neither the old men nor the fathers are able to provide an unambiguous and explicit male model. Masculinity is to a large degree demonstrated in arenas outside the village. Circumcision also reveals male connotations other than those observed by boys in everyday village interaction. The boys are exposed to

---

[9] My argument in this section is inspired by Horney's hypothesis as presented in "The Dread of Woman" (Horney, 1973b, pp. 133–146).

blood and pain, which was what men had to deal with as fierce pirates. The masculine role might also have had an ambivalent character. In the village men were usually docile. But during war and piracy they were fierce and aggressive, never frightened and never afraid of being killed, Bonerate men have told me. With the end of piracy the need for the painful circumcision ritual should be less strong than in earlier days.

Much ritual activity is directed toward ensuring future fertility. According to both male and female informants, the worst disaster a woman can experience is to be barren. If a marriage remains childless the blame is always attributed to the woman. But if no more children are conceived after a first child is born, the father is blamed for lacking virility.

Through all stages of the female circumcision, ritual symbols of fertility are explicitly present. The container-shaped coconut flowers attached to the wall, the eggs in the bed, and the throwing of rice are all familiar symbols of fertility. Also the white sheets may symbolize bridewealth and marriage. Further, it may be no coincidence that a renowned midwife is both the preferred ritual leader and the one who does the circumcision.

During female circumcision, social position is also symbolized. The color of the eggs indicate the social position of the girl. According to Bugis tradition, there should be seven colors representing the rainbow and the connection between this world and that of the spirits. Colors are, however, also markers of social position, thus only nobles were allowed to apply all colors (Paeni, personal communication, 1979). Also Miang Tuu villagers confirm that not long ago there were taboos about special foods and colors that could be used by Bonerate royalty only. Thus the ritual is a demonstration of the social position of the novices. The eggs at Jamilan's circumcision were of only four colors.

Miang Tuu female rituals confirm the findings of Judith Brown:

> First, female initiation rites occur in those societies in which the young girl does not leave the domestic unit of her parents after marriage. Second, those female initiation rites which subject the initiate to extreme pain are observed in those societies in which conditions in infancy and childhood result in a conflict of sex identity. Third, female initiation rites are found in those societies in which women make a notable contribution to subsistence activities. (Brown, 1963, pp. 849–851)

Bonerate marriage is predominantly uxorilocal. Throughout childhood, girls hang around their mothers; also after marriage, mother–daughter relations are warm and multiplex (Broch, 1988). Through childhood, girls are provided with models, which in a rather explicit way confront them with an unambiguous sex-role pattern. Girls experience confidence in their own sex from an early age; women are respected for their reproductive ability, for their productive skills in food processing, for ritual knowledge, and for their role as family treasurers. Thus, since the Miang Tuu girl experiences few identity problems in regard to her sex role, circumcision rituals serve to reinforce her sense of feminine identity. As the novice during the ritual, she appears as a symbol of femininity. She does not symbolize a female identity as experienced in the everyday village context; rather, she symbolizes an idealized component of the role repertoire stressing *malu* behavior. To be *malu* is an especially important component of female conduct, which embraces a wide spectrum of affects. To be *malu* is to be shy, to feel embarrassment, and also to carry connotations about losing face or feeling guilt (see also Lundstrom-Burghoorn, 1981). Sitting in the bed, the initiate is trained in screening out the activity around her. The room is teeming with stimuli, but she must ignore them for the sake of her *malu* presentation of self. "From a sense of self-control without loss of self-esteem comes a lasting sense of good will and pride" (Erikson, 1978, p. 228). The villagers, eating and talking, seem to ignore the girl, but at the same time she demonstrates to them the ideal of being *malu* (for instance, she looks down, does not enter conversation, and does not eat before all others have had their share). By their passive behavior toward the girl, the guests assure her sex-role identity and pride. In the modern village setting, to be *malu* is also connected to Islam. In everyday life, many of these rules are not followed strictly, but the ceremonies each time serve as reminders. When strangers arrive in Miang Tuu, women and girls are much more *malu* than otherwise.

Cooperation between the sexes is another theme that is repeated in different ways during the female circumcision ritual. (I have little knowledge of cooperation during male circumcision). It is an adolescent boy who mixes the *batiranga;* men and women cheer for her after circumcision; men carry her back to her mother's house, a young man shades her from the sun. This might have at least two interpretations. The young men further strengthen the female self by serving the girl, and the young girl symbolizes to the men community stability. It is to their women, the houses of wives and mothers, that men return after a voyage. There they are also supposed to find their women, who are not supposed to leave the home.

CHAPTER 5

The Docile Time of Puberty and Adolescence

Neither Child nor Adult

In this chapter I shall show how some of the conclusions reached in the analyses of Bonerate circumcision rituals—that is, that girls emerge with a less conflicting or more integrated, self identity, and that girls develop a greater confidence in their sex roles than boys—are supported by their adolescent behavior.

Melanie Klein has claimed that

> The onset of menstruation arouses strong anxiety in the girl. In addition to the various other meanings which it has and with which we are familiar it is, in the last resort, the outward and visible sign that the interior of her body and the children contained there have been totally destroyed. For this reason the development of a complete feminine attitude in girls takes longer and is beset with more difficulties than is the case with the boy in establishing his masculine position. (Klein, 1975, p. 85)

To Klein this situation applies to all girls during puberty regardless of the culture in which they live. Although she may have located some very important factors in understanding the psychosocial development of young women, the Bonerate material indicates that her assumption does not have cross-cultural validity. This does not say that primary or deep structure conflicts of Miang Tuu boys and girls are much different from those of their Western peers, but it means that the cultural mechanisms at their disposal for handling the problems are different in Miang Tuu. This allows Miang Tuu girls, at the conscious level at least, to follow a shorter path to feminine-role security than the boys follow to reach the same level of confidence in their self-identity.

Bonerate children were not expected to metamorphose from child to adult behavior as a result of the initiation ceremonies. After the children passed these ceremonies, they were not regarded as either physically or mentally mature. During the years following initiation and until adult status is recognized at marriage and the birth of the first child, the adolescents ideally should be reaching for a culturally accepted role and an integrated personal identity.

> The basic patterns of [this] identity must emerge from 1) the selective affirmation and repudiation of an individual's childhood identifications; and 2) the way in which the social process of the times identifies young individuals—at best recognizing them as persons who had to become the way they are and who, being the way they are, can be trusted. The community, in turn, feels recognized by the individual who cares to ask for such recognition. (Erikson, 1982, p. 72)

Here I shall claim that a sense of identity confusion is a normal condition of most adolescent Miang Tuu boys, whereas this is not obvious to the same degree with adolescent girls.

During the adolescent years, gender roles are more explicitly differentiated than at any other time in the life cycle of Miang Tuu villagers. Interestingly enough, the islanders do not seem to codify this with reference to an ideology of a division between male and female work. What happens in this particular context during these years has little influence on the sex-related division of adult labor. It is an observable fact that not only do adolescent boys engage in less work than their mothers and sisters, but they also work far less than their fathers. As will be remembered, Miang Tuu husbands take on their full share of household labor when they are home from sea. The adolescent boys are also in many ways less active than their younger peers. The daily life of adolescent boys is marked by an unfamiliar (by Bonerate standards) amount of leisure and a remarkably high level of passivity. They sit around chatting in the village. They are not discussing important political matters, nor are they training in rhetorical skills. They are relaxing to the point of boredom. The leisure is sometimes broken when a boy goes on an occasional fishing trip or works for a while on a swidden. The boys do not like to help their mothers as husbands help their wives, nor do they work together with their fathers as often as their sisters assist their mothers. During adolescence, a pattern of mild avoidance is established between fathers and sons. This avoidance is especially at force during work and is referred to as a sign of mutual respect.

Some days the boys of this age complain that there is little for them to do in the village. They become restless and want to get off to sea. They share daydreams about how they will return to the village rich in money and goods. But the reality of such dreams belongs to the past, when young men could return with a fortune earned from piracy and smuggling. Nowadays crew members do not earn much at sea. Meanwhile, the boys still in the village, perhaps regarded as a little too young for *perahu* sailing, are allowed to take it easy. Others who have returned from their first trip but are still unmarried, also have a "good time." Now they are becoming concerned about the issue of getting married. There are few potential wives in the village, so most boys realize that they will have to marry into a new social environment. Although most trust the efforts and the decision of their parents, who will often be assisted by *ibu* and *bapak lingkung,* some boys say that it is easier to find a bride on Java or in other faraway places. But even though it may also be cheaper, such a marriage is the last alternative, only relevant if it proves too difficult to arrange a marriage on Bonerate.

Because social status is dependent on the social position of the wife, boys would be able to marry better if they could manage to accumulate wealth that may substitute for their lack of social position. Therefore some boys say they want to delay their marriage until they manage to save some money—a common rationalization where it is difficult to find a marriageable partner. No one had earned significant money as a sailor in recent years, but after some years marriage is arranged anyway.

Miang Tuu boys seem to express an incestuous fixation on their mothers and sisters. They love their mothers and speak tenderly of all female household members. Often the other village girls are also referred to as sisters to be protected from both physical and moral dangers. Adolescent boys and girls mingle, but overt sexual passes seem absent. They walk together in mixed groups but are never observed in pairs. They talk or sometimes sit down to listen to music.

Bonerate men and adolescent boys are indeed concerned about their own virility and fear impotence (Broch, 1983, pp. 154–155). This is not too surprising when we consider the strength of the mother–child bond in terms of fixation. Widespread behavioral similarities in incestuous fixation on mothers are frequently observed in South and Southeast Asia. The incestuous fixation on the mother results in strong feelings of sexual guilt, which in turn is the source of a shame that may often lead to impotence. Also, in accordance with a Freudian model (Freud, 1974, pp. 63–65), Bonerate men, so they say, do not feel it would be right to engage in extramarital relations or premarital sex with Bonerate girls and women. But to have such relations with the pretty but bad, possibly Christian, women on the Moluccas or the prostitutes of Surabaya is a totally different matter. In fact, the homecoming sailors often brag about such experiences at their return from a voyage. Thus they seem more worried about sexual inadequacy and impotence in their relationship with their wives and potential brides than with the girls in faraway ports. With the latter one can always have sex and with them sex is easy, the sailors say.

Adolescent boys sometimes openly express their wish to marry within the village because they regard it best to stay close to the natal home. But, unfortunately, there are few possibilities for such arrangements. Many boys seem to feel uncomfortable about having to move away from their natal, maternal household. Both girls and boys persist in their love for their mother through childhood and far beyond puberty. Instead of roaring upheavals against their parents and community during the time of puberty, Miang Tuu adolescents show passionate interest in the ideological values of adjustment to social norms of behavior. They show great devotion to their parents and in particular, as noted, to their mothers. They readily express confidence in the decisions their parents make on their behalf. Or to put it differently, they never show disagreement, never argue, and never openly express bad feeling toward their parents. This devotion and dependence on parental figures is also reflected in the villagers' relations with *ibu* and *bapak lingkung,* to whom they regularly turn for advice in various contexts. Adult villagers seek advice from them in such matters as finding spouses for their children, determining the bride-price, arranging ritually important feasts, solving marital conflicts, and handling children. Adolescents sometimes ask *ibu* and *bapak*

lingkung to intervene if they experience difficulties in social relations, and boys ask help in finding a *perahu* they can join as crew
members. The villagers tend to regard *ibu* and *bapak lingkung* as
idealized parental figures, in contrast to authority figures farther
away, which are generally described as tyrannical and untrust-
worthy. In this conceptualization of different authority figures, we
can rediscover the child's suspicion and fear of strangers confirmed in adult behavior.

For the girls, the time of puberty is somewhat different.
Whereas their brothers have to prove manhood at sea, the girls are
already mature women in miniature. They have acquired the prerequisite skills for their female roles and are busily engaged in all
kinds of work in close company with their mothers and sisters.
When they menstruate, they wash before dawn and after sunset,
but that is the normal practice of all women most days. Girls often
stay in bed a day or two because of menstrual pains, but they are
not secluded.[1] Their brothers and fathers may see them and sit
down to chat, although strangers are not allowed to come close.
Women, of course, are free to see the menstruating girl. She is not
regarded as contaminating and may, if she herself feels fit, help in
the preparation of food for all household members. Thus the adolescent girl demonstrates both physically and socially her transitional stage to adulthood in a way that is impossible for boys.
Emotionally, however, both the adolescent girl and boy are still
immature. The villagers believe that the occasional display of
emotional behavior that is present throughout childhood will first
disappear when the individuals are fully grown, that is, when they

---

[1] Karen Horney found in her clinical work that the appearance of premenstrual tension was
particularly strong where the desire for a child was great, but at the same time strong personal defenses against procreation were present (Horney, 1973a, pp. 99–106). To my
knowledge, her hypothesis has never been tested cross-culturally in view of culturally constituted defense mechanisms. Without claiming to have tested her hypothesis in this way, I
will draw attention to an interesting finding: the apparent difference between Hare Indians
in North Canada and Miang Tuu villagers. Hare Indian adolescent women claim that they
do not suffer from premenstrual pain and tension. Among the Hare Indians, children born
before marriage are not stigmatized and neither are their mothers. Among Miang Tuu girls,
children are much wanted, but positively not before marriage. If a child should be born outside of marriage, the young mother would disgrace not only herself but also her relatives
and the whole village. Bonerate women claim that premenstrual pain and tension disappear
at marriage. This statement seems to hold true according to observed female behavior in
Miang Tuu. However, further and more focused investigations are needed before claims to
the cross-cultural validity of Horney's hypothesis can be made.

themselves become parents. However, adolescents are corrected when they act childishly; they are told to "smarten up" when they lose their tempers and, for instance, harshly criticize their younger siblings.

Most girls will remain in Miang Tuu or close to the village even after their marriage. The parents and the girl herself find the thought that she might move away from Bonerate disturbing. Miang Tuu girls do not believe in love at first sight; it does not apply in their situation. They believe that love is what develops between husband and wife in the years following their wedding. The girls expect that the first years are the hardest to get through, but they also claim that marital conflicts during this period are reduced because their husbands are off to sea for long periods. The girls do not seem to dream about ideal partners and are not overtly concerned about whom they will marry. Miang Tuu girls seem to trust the decision of their parents and agree that, after all, they know best. We should also remember that divorce is almost absent from Bonerate; and not a single case is reported or can be remembered to have happened in Miang Tuu.

In spite of what both adolescent girls and boys say, there are indeed indications that they are quite concerned about whom they eventually will marry. Girls should be virgins at the time of their first marriage, and their chastity is of concern to the girl, her peers, and all adult villagers.

Adolescents are also much concerned about their appearance. Both boys and girls groom their hair and try to dress impressively. Boys returning from sea dress themselves in black shoes, bright shirts, and fashionably cut slacks. They also bring home colorful *sarongs* for their mothers and sisters. Girls, if possible, put aside money for months in order to buy a skirt or a new *sarong*. They love to try on the few pairs of high-heeled shoes that are in the village. Girls from the poorer households borrow clothes from their more affluent friends when they want to show off. The girls who can afford to care make sure not to expose their faces to the sun and apply a cooling dough to their skin to keep a light complexion (see the description of female circumcision in Chapter 4). Likewise, they cover up their hair so that the sun will not bleach its color. When adolescents a few times during the year visit another Bonerate village to attend a ceremony or a feast, they take great pains to be beautiful and graceful. The boys say openly that they like to watch the girls to see whom they would like to marry; perhaps they afterwards even offer a mild suggestion to their own parents. When asked about their own behavior, the girls giggle and only reluctantly admit that they like to watch the boys for the same reason.

The importance both girls and boys place on their own appearance and that of their potential spouses and the keen interest they express in what they believe to be the custom of love marriages elsewhere contrast sharply with the values their parents say are most important. Bonerate parents say that the potential spouse for their child should have inner qualities such as emotional control, should be industrious, and should not be a gambler in economic affairs.

The parents also say they can better deal with the question of incest than their children, who do not always have all the social information on such issues. And, of course, they firmly stress that social equality has to be established between bride and groom. Love marriages are not regarded as good, because they are based on too much emotional attachment, which is supposed to be of short endurance. Both Miang Tuu boys and girls quite consistently follow the recommendations of their elders in the choice of spouses; it is clear that a detachment from parental authority has not developed during the time of adolescence.

Haisa and Mellog

Haisa is an older sister of Owati, and thus a daughter of *ibu* and *bapak lingkung*. Mellog is her cousin, his mother being one of *ibu*'s younger sisters. Mellog's father has the reputation of being a merry man and a strong worker. He is well liked by most villagers. Haisa was approximately fifteen years old, and Mellog approximately one year younger than she. He had not been off to sea but hoped to join a *perahu* shortly after my departure from the island. That this hope might well come true was confirmed by his father who told me that it was now time for Mellog to go to sea. As we shall see, Mellog also prepared himself for life on the sea.

I shall give some ethnographic examples from the daily life of adolescent Miang Tuu girls and boys as illustrated by these two cousins. They are not completely representative because both were from the more affluent village households and were perhaps among the most industrious of their peers. This was particularly true of Mellog. Yet they should well serve to illuminate aspects of adolescent behavior in the present context.

Mellog expressed the typical emergent role and identity frustration of adolescent Miang Tuu boys. He complained about having too little to do in the village, where there were too few age-mates, village life was dull, and nothing ever happened. He often talked about how much he longed for the sea. Almost every day he walked down to the beach with his bamboo fishing pole. He enjoyed joining me for fishing but rarely went fishing with his father. Sometimes he helped his mother or father in various agricultural work. He helped his mother with the harvesting of cassava and his father with bringing home corn and other crops from the fields. The villagers remarked when Mellog appeared with his heavy loads that he was indeed growing up to resemble his father. Around the house he helped his mother and older sisters at the large mortars pestling corn or peas, or he would pound dry cassava into crude flour. Mellog, a strong boy, brought home loads of dry firewood. He climbed the coconut palms as fast as any and harvested nuts and cut loose old leaves with his *parang*.

Because Mellog had two younger siblings, he seldom had to fetch water or look after his youngest brother. Occasionally he played with the much younger village children. He seemed to like the company of Owati, but never played with her for long and never spent time with girls his own age, such as Haisa. There simply were no other boys his age permanently residing in the village. He hung around those a little older when they returned from their voyages to listen to stories of their adventures. At night he visited the homes of other villagers and listened to their conversations. He seldom interrupted discussions without being asked and kept a respectful distance from adults. Before his voice had found its mature new pitch, he acted embarrassed when his voice cracked. This was apparent when he talked to adults and lost track of his own thoughts whenever squeaky sounds appeared in his flow of speech. When this happened, he often stopped in the middle of his sentence before he had reached the point he wanted to make. I viewed this as a sign of frustration that interfered with his efforts to gain recognition through participation in adult conversation. The cracks in his voice undermined his ego strivings toward self-esteem by denying him the illusion of having developed beyond childhood. This conflict was an internal one, since nobody teased him for this, and the attention of those to whom he spoke did not waver due to his voice cracks.

When the villagers visited one another they always seated themselves according to their social positions. But when young boys returned from sea, they were temporarily granted central seats alongside *kepala lingkung* to inform him about prices on copra and so forth. After a few days the adolescents retreated to their peripheral places and returned the more important seats to the village elders or other holders of high social position.

Mellog was polite, obedient, and well liked by his elders. Once after he had joined his father on a voyage to Ujung Pandang to sell green peas, he was given much attention. In the evenings he told about his experiences. He was especially surprised at how many white people he had seen in the large city. They could be spotted in all places, he said. His audience nodded and listened, but when more adults arrived, Mellog had to retreat to a less central seat and when any of the adults needed something—for instance, tobacco—Mellog was asked to leave and get it.

One evening Mellog came to the house to talk to me. No tea, or rather hot water, was prepared for him. That was an explicit signal that the female household members still did not regard him as an adult. Mellog said he was looking forward to *bulan sebelas* (November), because at that time Miang Tuu would be *rame* (lively with parties and fun, with lots to do and see). In November most of the sailors are expected to return from sea and stay in the village for two or three months.

Mellog also said he enjoyed clearing brush to prepare new swiddens; sometimes he joined his mother in this work. But his father would not let him work together with him, because the work was too exhausting for Mellog. As indicated earlier, fathers and adolescent sons rarely work together. Actually Mellog cooperated more with his father than boys returning from their first voyages did with their fathers. However, in the context of *gotong royong,* which is a common way to organize the clearing of new swiddens, fathers may send their adolescent sons as substitues for themselves to fulfill the household's obligation within the work team. Mellog had participated in large *gotong royong* parties to clear new land for cultivation. At these times, he was served food together with the adult members of the work group. Thus we have to question Mellog's father's explanation as to why the two did not work side by side on such work tasks. The reason was not a lack of strength in Mellog, but rather the culturally instituted father–son contextual pattern of avoidance.

The evening when Mellog visited me was in the middle of Ramadan. Although Mellog's father was among the few in the village to adhere to the prescribed fast, his son ate as usual. That was another sign of his context-related status as a child.

For a while, Mellog walked every morning to work in *ibu kota*. In this context he was performing the job of an adult man, helping the *perahu* builders of Bonerate to complete and outfit a new *perahu*. This was also the boat on which he would be a crew member on her maiden voyage. It was regarded as important that all crew members know how *perahus* are built, as eventually they would make all necessary repairs on the vessels they sailed.

One day Mellog relaxed outside his home in Miang Tuu. His father walked toward him, carrying Mellog's youngest sibling, who had just learned to walk. When he was put down, the toddler started to crawl in the dust. Mellog carefully put his brother in an upright position and made him walk. He was indeed patient with the toddler who now tried in vain to reach a leaf of a young coconut sapling. Mellog bent the leaf down in order to let his brother play. After a while the toddler approached his big brother, who picked him up, placed him on his lap, and patted him. Mellog groomed the hair of his little brother, removing a couple of dry straws from his front hair.

Mellog's everyday behavior can be interpreted as a continuous experimentation in identity potentials. He was not yet adult, but he strived to put childhood behind him. Sometimes he comfortably regressed to play with young children during the day, but again strived for adult recognition through interaction with his seniors in the evening. Interestingly enough, he seemed mature and secure in the emotional control that is regarded as crucial to the achievement of an adult status. A polite boy, Mellog was never observed to lose his temper. But this was not enough. He remained in an ambiguous position, drawing benefits and restrictions from the worlds of both children and adults. A final transition to adult status could not be achieved before he returned as an acknowledged sailor after becoming a *perahu* crew member, eventually married, and had children. Alternative roads to adult recognition may exist, but the elements I have described are among the more important in the lives of most adolescent Miang Tuu boys.

Let us now turn to Haisa. Her days were busy; little in her workload or household tasks separated her role from that of adult Miang Tuu women. Still, she had not yet achieved the status of adulthood. What seemed to prohibit her transition to adult status again is related to some few but rather important social factors. Crucial elements in this context are related to sex. The adolescent girl is culturally denied heterosexual intimacy. Premarital sex is not tolerated. The villagers say this is important to prevent violations of incest rules and to protect the honor of the girls and their relatives. Adult status and recognition is not a matter of physical age and maturity but is closely tied to motherhood. Other girls at Haisa's age had already married and accordingly achieved adult status through marriage and motherhood. The villagers say that girls used to marry earlier in the old days. Also, girls of the more affluent households tended to marry later than others.

Haisa was usually the first member of the household to rise in the morning. When it was still dark, she lit a wick stuck into a tiny bottle containing paraffin, the house's lamp. Then she moved over to the firehouse or kitchen. Here she made fire on the open fireplace to prepare hot water or occasionally tea. If, for instance, her father could be expected home soon from a night's fishing, or if he was due to leave for an early fishing expedition, some food might be prepared in addition to the water. This first meal of the day had the character of a snack. Boiled pumpkins, deep-fried bananas, some boiled cassava, or even a few cookies could be served. In most households, however, no food was made at this time of the day. The first regular meal was served around ten o'clock in the morning. Between noon and two o'clock, hot water or perhaps tea was served again, occasionally with some snacks, such as those mentioned, to accompany the first glass of water in the morning. Finally, just after sunset, it was time for supper. Hot dishes were prepared for both the morning meal and supper. Lukewarm water always accompanied the major meals. Usually the food in Haisa's household would be a mixture of partly ground corn and rice. Most villagers served unmixed corn and cassava only. If available, fish, sea urchins, pumpkins, papaya flowers, various leaves, and lugworms, would be eaten along with either the corn, cassava, or rice that constitute the basic ingredients. The side dishes took quite a long time and much attention to prepare on the fireplace. Haisa made most of the food prepared in the household. On an average it took her from two to two-and-a-half hours to prepare each of the two daily meals. Sometimes she was assisted by her mother or sisters. But when they were working on the swiddens, Haisa was in complete charge in the firehouse. Among her other routine tasks were grinding corn and rice, sweeping the floors, tidying the beds and rolling up sleeping mats, fetching water, washing clothes, and cutting firewood. She often got help in many of these activities from her younger sister and other small assistants, but it was she who had the responsibility to see that things were done in the right time. Haisa also joined other household members outdoors as they cultivated and gathered food. During the peaks of the agricultural cycle she worked on the swiddens, and she occasionally went along to gather seashore animals. However, Haisa definitely spent much less time outdoors than her mother and two married sisters.

During my stay in the village, Halima, Haisa's older sister, taught her to do embroidery on a sewing machine. Whenever she was free from other work, she sat down at the sewing machine and kept busy. Because there were few such machines in the village and few women had time free for sewing, this was high status work. The two sisters sewed for several villagers in addition to meeting the household's needs. When they were busy at the machine, the room was usually crowded with young girls who watched their skills with admiration.

Haisa told me that she did not like outdoor work, and she said that it was good for her complexion to remain inside to avoid the tanning effect of the burning sun! Her image of the ideally pretty dream girl was one with light complexion, dark eyes, and long, straight, black hair; her body should be quite fat. It is great to be fat, to have a rounded form and a large bosom. Gold jewelry in plenty, of course, European-styled dresses, and high-heeled shoes also enhance the beauty of women!

Apparently Haisa enjoyed her work. When she prepared food or swept the floors, she usually hummed a tune. Her laughter was also often heard in Miang Tuu. One day an extremely funny incident happened in the village that made Haisa and all the watching villagers laugh. An adolescent girl stumbled and the bucket of water she carried on her head fell down so that the girl got soaking wet. While everybody laughed, the unfortunate girl explained with a smile how she had caught her foot on a stick that lay on the ground.

In addition to being cheerful, Haisa was strong-minded. She did not like others to interfere with her business. When I once brought some gifts for the women of the household on returning from a trip to Bali, she was quick to get hold of what she liked the best. Haisa distributed what she did not want for herself between her two older sisters! It also happened that her sisters got things Haisa wanted, and she made them give her those too. The sisters said they hardly dared deny her what she wanted because they knew few others who could be more furious than Haisa.

Occasionally Haisa tended her sister's toddler. She was kind to the child and liked to pet her for a while. But she also loved to tease the tiny one when she was crying. Haisa made faces to the crybaby while she herself laughed with all her might. Haisa was also the only one to correct her brother Leipi when he acted unpleasantly. Haisa was once reprimanded for this by her mother and father, but she responded with a smile that she would try to improve, but after all, the youngsters only got what they deserved! Besides this, Haisa treated the house cat more roughly than did any other household member.

Once when Haisa was sick, probably with malaria, she was shaken by an unpleasant experience. Her parents were off to Java; her two elder sisters slept in the next house so Haisa and I were staying home alone. One day a young barefoot doctor from Java arrived in the village to sell medicines. He came to the house of *kepala lingkung* and said that he would spend two or three days in Miang Tuu to complete his business. Because Haisa lay sick in bed, her two older sisters prepared food for the stranger and me. The next morning when I was still half asleep, I noticed the stranger walking into the room where Haisa slept. A moment later he came out. I got up, and when I returned from the morning bath at the well, shared the breakfast ordered by the stranger. He ate hastily five eggs that he bought the night before and told me that he should have given Haisa some medicine. However, he got to his feet, grabbed his belongings, and left the house in a hurry while he murmured, "Stupid women in this backward village." He had barely left when Yobaida and Halima, Haisa's sisters, ran into the room and cried out:

> That man is a bad human. He wanted to ruin Haisa. If he were to stay longer, we would have prepared no more food for him. While we were in the kitchen this morning, he sneaked up to Haisa where she was lying down on her *tikar* [sleeping mat]. She called for us, but we did not hear her cry. If we had known that he would have dared to come, we would have been there, right at her side. But how could we know? There he stood, looking right at her. Poor Haisa, she has a fever too [*sakit panas*]. She covered herself with an extra *sarong* and kicked at him. He is a bad man. If our father had been here, he would surely have killed that Javanese man. How awful! He would never again have been able to return to Bonerate. But you must not tell this to anybody. If you do so, you will only make things worse. Poor Haisa, she is crying in the kitchen.

Yobaida continued: "Last night I thought I should sleep in this house, in this room, but I did not trust that man. If we had only known how bad he was, he would never have slept in the house." During the day Halima and Yobaida told other women what happened, and they were all shocked by the unheard-of behavior of the stranger. Some hours later Halima asked me why I did not stop the man. I answered that I was still very sleepy and never realized that Haisa was no longer alone. "That was what we thought," Halima said. "He knew you were sleeping." The next day Haisa's uncles also knew, having been told by their wives. One of them wanted to talk to me about the incident. He was angry and said he never before thought such disgusting behavior possible. If he had learned about this while the man was still in the village, he would have had to do something. But as it turned out, he said, nothing really disastrous had happened. He also wanted me to confirm that I did not know anything before the man left the house. He told me that he had spoken to other men in Miang Tuu, and they had all agreed that if this Javanese man ever returns to the village, he shall be beaten and made to run away. Finally he informed me that he had told his wife that if Harald had been awake, he would surely have done something. After this talk all the villagers seemed to share the idea that if I had understood a little earlier what had happened in the house that morning, I would have killed that man!

Haisa's behavior shows that adolescent girls have to struggle with psychological stress within an idiosyncratic as well as an idiomatic context. The time of puberty does not create strong reactions against the cultural norms, such as those related to shame and honor, that are guarded by parents and the adult villagers. Indeed, the adolescents strive to conform in order to gain respect and adult recognition.

The lack of severe generational conflict at the time of adolescence should not be surprising. Psychoanalytic methods have shown that conflicts during adolescence to a large degree have their roots in early childhood, usually in the oedipal phase of development. Later conflicts are merely new versions of the original (Brenner, 1974, p. 223). In the Miang Tuu case we have seen that conflicts during the oedipal phase generally seem to be successfully suppressed and do not reemerge at the time of adolescence.

The adolescents of course, like all other islanders, know that they will not be regarded as adult before their marriage, but they strive to be accepted as full community members in as many contexts as possible. When the unmarried girls seem confident in their social roles of female power and importance and appear generally obedient to their elders, this does not mean that their lives are free from psychic stress. Rather, everyday behavior shows that psychic conflicts are displaced and repressed. Conformity to a docile, nonaggressive behavior has its psychic costs. Haisa managed to disguise much anger and frustration in an everyday context by means of displacement. I interpret her aggressiveness toward the household's cat, the teasing of her niece, and her strict correction of Leipi as various indications of displaced aggression. I am not able to pinpoint the primary sources of her aggression; what is important here is that she finds culturally accepted ways to express herself. This is also easier because she is still not regarded as emotionally mature and is not supposed to be so in the view of the villagers because she has not yet gained adult status.

When Haisa was embarrassed and insulted by the Javanese man, nothing would probably have happened if she had not told her sisters about the incident. But Haisa could not be completely sure that nobody had noticed. The probability that someone indeed knew and her feeling of guilt even if nobody found out were too much for her to deal with alone. By telling her sisters, she surely knew that they would carry the news further. Thus her guilt was transformed to shame—a shame she shared with all household members and even with all villagers. When the accident became public knowledge, her guilt was radically reduced by the massive support of all villagers. All blame was tied to the stranger from Java; the villagers got new evidence confirming their suspicion of all strangers. Although the honor of Miang Tuu girls is primarily the concern of their close relatives, all villagers feel responsible to help protect all local unmarried girls. It is striking to notice that in spite of the strong position of Miang Tuu women, they in this situation look to their men for help. When fate turns on them, all villagers regardless of sex turn to their mothers (if possible) to seek nurturant understanding. But in the case of Haisa, when her honor was at stake and physical violence may have been required to prevent disgrace, it was her father that was missed. It is likely that if Haisa's mother had been home, she would have been the first to know, but she would probably have informed her husband.[2] The social honor and position that men gain from their women must be protected. But the women are also concerned. If they inform the men, they know that the men will have to respond, perhaps with violent aggression. Once they are informed by the women, the men who might wish not to know or not to take action are in a difficult position. The very act of informing a man about such an incident is a culturally sanctioned demand for some kind of action.

But heavy burdens are also placed on the adolescent girl. She must give no one a reason to gossip about her not being *malu*. Rumors may easily create shame, and a shamed girl throws shame on all members of the household to which she belongs. In the village girls are safe, but whenever they want to go beyond the village, they make sure they have female company. Thus, adolescent girls never work alone on the swiddens, but always in small groups. Unmarried girls do not even dare to walk alone ten minutes' distance to fetch bananas or papaya from a garden beyond the village grounds.

In many ways sex roles are expressed most explicitly during the time of adolescence when marriage is approaching. Miang Tuu

---

[2] This guess is quite hypothetical because if Haisa's parents had been home, the stranger would not have had an opportunity to be alone with the girl.

gender ideology is an elaboration of a theme described in many Southeast Asian cultures. In addition to the acknowledgment of gender complementarity in social life, women and especially mothers are held in high esteem. Mattulada, for instance, says about the Bugis, one of Bonerate's close neighbors:

> The brother has a strong feeling towards his sister, that is, he feels called upon to protect her in any situation. This is based upon the notion that the sister is the living representation of his mother, the highest symbol of honor within the family connected with *siri* dignity. (Mattulada, 1982, p. 17)

On Bonerate, a man's social position and honor are dependent on his mother and later his wife. But during adolescence the young man cannot remain only a passive supporter of women and thereby gain acknowledgment as a man. He ought to take command by carrying out relevant household obligations. He should show respect for his father and all community members who rank above him in social status. He should be supportive of his mother and supportive of and nurturant toward his siblings. The adolescent boy also actively seeks to expose his emergent masculinity by caring about his appearance, excelling in masculine activities such as fishing and searching for *lola* snails, and showing off his eagerness to prove his manhood as a member of a *perahu* crew.

I have pointed out some social and psychological problems most Miang Tuu adolescents face before they gain adult status. Whereas boys are insecure in their gender role performances and struggle to be allowed to carry out much adult work, girls are already performing most tasks required of adult women. This contributes to a more secure sex identity in girls than in boys of that age. Whereas a mild pattern of father–son avoidance develops, girls continue to work close to their mothers. Boys have to go away from the island to achieve adult status; girls stay behind and do not have to be exposed to the frightening and exciting outer world to get adult recognition. Girls are less concerned than boys about adult recognition. They seem to be more patient and feel less hurry to get married than their brothers do. Girls also often express anxiety at the mere thought of being separated from their mothers for a long time. The honor of girls is dependent on restrictions in their movement. Boys gain honor through their sisters' behavior and their own dangerous voyages.

However, to finally gain adult status both boys and girls are dependent on each other. They have to unite through marriage, raise children, and direct their efforts toward the common goal of the development of a viable household of their own. When the first child is born, their own childhood is finally ended. From that moment on, childlike behavior in the new parents is regarded as culturally deviant and indeed subject to public gossip and condemnation.

CONCLUSION

Growing Up in Miang Tuu

This book has focused on how children are brought up and develop within the social context of Miang Tuu on Bonerate. We have described how tiny humans become talking, thinking, believing, valuing, and acting members of the village society and Bonerate culture. The chapters examine the ways children gradually acquire the necessary skills and learn to think, act, and feel appropriately—that is, how they want to act and must act if the cultural system is to be maintained. In covering certain parts of this process that are typical for Miang Tuu, we have emphasized what older people and parents do to and for younger people to make them grow up properly. Much cultural teaching remains implicit and is in many instances not a matter of explicit intentions carried out purposely by the caretakers. The young people react to their environment in many ways; here we have stressed their observations and speculations about what they learn.

The social setting gives somewhat different options to individuals who are raised in different households. Although the social position of one's parents is certainly important in this connection, other factors such as birth order and personal resources also significantly influence much or most interaction. This interest in individual differences is not an end in itself but appears necessary to grasp the nature of Bonerate culture. Studying individual variation helps us to understand why some community members are better at what they do than others; why some are more likely to choose certain roles; and why some, for instance, appear happier and better adjusted, more innovative, and more eager to learn new ways.

Many important messages of great cultural significance are never expressed verbally or made explicit by direct instructions.

But sentiments, ritual, work, and play are always present, all part of a Miang Tuu ethos. Because much of the culture is transmitted rather effortlessly (which is not the same as a transmission free from social or psychological costs), it would be difficult for the children not to learn their culture. In spite of this formulation I do not view cultural transmission as an "automatic" process which produces cultural blueprints. Bonerate culture is by no means static, but so far changes have emerged gradually, at a rate that has permitted cultural integration, and this is one of the reasons a study of Bonerate children is particularly fascinating. This is especially true of Miang Tuu residents, who even by Bonerate islanders are regarded as constituting an isolated village community. This relative cultural stability is important to our understanding of what it is like to grow up in Miang Tuu. This is a situation that differs from most societies in our rapidly developing modern world.

Although I have emphasized differing individual options within this small village of fewer than 200 residents and Miang Tuu also differs slightly from other Bonerate villages, all islanders nevertheless adhere to a common Bonerate culture. It may even be possible to claim that Miang Tuu villagers represent a version of what the well-known Indonesian anthropologist Koentjaraningrat has designated an Indonesian peasant mentality. His definition of *peasants* includes people whose economic systems are based on agriculture (cultivation of land, animal husbandry, and fishing) in which simple technology and nonspecialized labor are utilized to produce food. According to Koentjaraningrat, peasants also feel that they are part of the lower strata of a culture whose upper strata, located in urban areas, are considered to be more refined and civilized. This peasant mentality is based on cultural values that are described as follows: In principle, Indonesian peasants (especially in Java) regard life as a bad thing, full of sins, and full of difficulties and dangers. However, this does not mean that they must withdraw from life and retreat for instance to Javanese mysticism or meditation; rather they feel an obligation to realize life by acting with "carefulness" and by doing their best through their own efforts.

Indonesian peasants work for a living and where possible, also for position. Because they are very poor, their attention is concentrated on the present and not on the future. Only occasionally do they think of the past, which according to legends told by their elders, was an era of greatness. In general, nature does not terrify them. If occasionally there are natural disasters such as volcanic eruptions, floods and so forth, these are accepted as bad fate, caused by accident or coincidence. Neither do they fear insects which destroy their crops: they know how to overcome such disasters. Even if occasionally they are not able to overcome them, they need not die of hunger because of the existence of the *gotong royong* ("mutual self-help") system which also gives them a deep sense of security. . . . They must be conscious that their lives depend on others. Therefore they must always cultivate good relationships with others. (Koentjaraningrat, 1988, pp. 110–111)

On the most general level some of the elements Koentjaraningrat points out as typical of an Indonesian peasant mentality might also constitute part of the cultural matrix Miang Tuu children are exposed to from birth and throughout their life cycles. But if I should try to single out what might appear endemic to a pattern of Miang Tuu socialization, I would focus on the matrifocal emphasis and the particular ways this is handled within the community. In this book I have tried to show the importance of early socialization for the development and elaboration of sex roles. There are always important differences in the growing up processes of boys and girls. For boys, there is an obligatory move from the women's side of society in order to gain recognition of manhood. In matrilocal societies, a shift from the mother's house to that of the wife is also part of normal development. I have argued that in the present context the transition to adult status is generally less complicated for girls than boys.

The book is arranged according to a chronological developmental model, with Chapter 1 focusing on the Miang Tuu children. Who children are and how long individuals may remain children are defined by adults. This is also true in Miang Tuu. Generally the adult population evaluates child activities as proper conduct for the various developmental stages. Healthy children of most cultures do, however, test and explore many rules and norms of conduct advocated by their elders. We cannot therefore assume a priori that the children and their caretakers agree on all issues related to the definition of childhood and children's activities, play, and work.

Where cultural and social changes are occurring at a high speed, "or too fast," parents feel frustrated because they are unsure about "the best way" for their children's education. In Miang Tuu both children and parents seem confident about the future.

Miang Tuu villagers have no preference in the sex of their children. More than 60 percent of all children born in Miang Tuu die before they are three years old. The overall attention during the first years is directed toward the survival of the baby. The infant must be named properly in order to thrive and be happy. An infant's cry is usually regarded as a cry for food, but it may also be interpreted as an indication of a badly chosen name. If so, a new name must be presented to the newborn, who is regarded as very fragile and not yet quite human. If this creature is offended in any way, it is likely to die. At approximately three to five months of age this first critical phase in the newborn's life ends and a named baby has made its entrance to the village community.

Chapter 2 describes infancy and the early years. Generally Miang Tuu villagers agree that babies, toddlers, and the youngest children should have their way and not be punished for misbehavior. Because infants are referred to as *bodoh*—stupid or not responsible for their actions—correction of their behavior seems meaningless. Likewise, Miang Tuu parents do not believe in rational arguments to teach their youngest children what is right and wrong or safe and dangerous. According to Bonerate islanders, young children lack the ability to reason because of their insufficient experience. Miang Tuu infants and toddlers are sheltered against pain-provoking experiences. In spite of these efforts, it is impossible to guard babies from bites from insects, for instance. This may add to an early conception of the dichotomy between a hostile or ambiguous environment and a friendly and reliable community.

The father, when he is home on the island, demonstrates much nurturant behavior toward his youngest children. This, and the fact that he is contributing to filling the infant's and young child's needs and also serving as a primary socializer, makes the expectations of both parents similar in some important ways. Both parents are significant in the early emotional constitution of their boys and girls.

Weaning is gradual and not forced upon the baby. During the first two years, lack of bowel and bladder control is interpreted as another manifestation of the *bodoh* nature of the youngest children. Miang Tuu villagers agree that most early child development is a natural accomplishment that will be mastered in due time. Some children take their first steps before they are one year old, while others do not control motor movements at the age of three. Girls often both walk and speak earlier than boys. Miang Tuu children, however, develop verbal skills relatively late. This may be related to the social environment, which offers few incentives to encourage such development. Neither adults nor older children talk much to babies and toddlers, but instead express their care by being close and by hugging and kissing the tiny ones. The severe distress that is observed when babies and toddlers are on rare occasions left alone seems to continue into adulthood. Bedtime and other rituals of safe passage give the child and parents a feeling of security.

Adults are supposed to control their emotions in most situations and contexts. The culturally specific child handling and rearing practices at Bonerate provide a setting where the baby is exposed to little aggression. The socialization of the youngest children is mild and gentle. Toddlers are rarely left alone. Before the age of five girls and boys are treated alike in most daily contexts.

Chapter 3, Miang Tuu Childhood, shows how socialization processes gradually give the children an emergent understanding of which values the society, through its adult members, regards as most important to guide social interaction. When children still do not master the preferred codes of interaction, this is sometimes used as an argument to keep them away from many activities and situations.

In most societies, when children have great freedom to experiment with roles and behavioral limits of tolerance, this is due to many circumstances. When for example the sanctions from parents and playmates are incompatible, children often change groups of reference. Usually this does not lead to frustrations that are too difficult to handle. Even young children learn that the different arenas have their own rules. What the child is not allowed to do in one place at a certain time may be possible in another situation and under different circumstances. This means that needs and wishes that cannot be fulfilled at once must be postponed or perhaps compensated for at some other time. This training in tolerance of delayed wish fulfillment takes many forms and is indeed one of the most general and important elements of all socialization processes.

Bonerate childhood is generally free and allows for leisure. Birth, sickness, intercourse, and death are all part of daily village life and the children are not barred from these events. Sex play between boys and girls seems absent, and even the idea of such play provokes abhorrent feelings among the villagers. Miang Tuu children have more time available than most children today, as they do not attend schools and their parents do not force many assignments on their children. Generally girls and boys play together, children of different ages mix freely, and they are rarely observed to play by themselves.

While adults consider that children mostly play, they also assist their parents. Many children's activities are regarded as work by the youngsters, and indeed it is often difficult to separate work from play in descriptions and analyses of their activities.

Play in Miang Tuu is generally noncompetitive; winners are not singled out and there is little or no emphasis on who is performing better or worse than others. True games are absent. The children have few toys; for instance, no one owns dolls or toy cars. Imitation play is infrequent, probably because the children are generally well informed about what their parents do, are allowed to assist in many ways, and also do most tasks for real, just as their parents do. Exceptions are when boys imitate war dances and girls imitate possession-trance rituals. These are activities that children are not free to join in the real context.

Aggression is seldom expressed explicitly during play, except when children play with live animals.

Social and material resources are unevenly distributed among the children of the different village households; these differences derive from the status of the child's parents.

The return home of the village's sailors is a time of great expectation and happiness to the children who are old enough to remember their father, although it might be a somewhat traumatic experience to those who do not. A lot of goodies are distributed throughout the village, and the children are allowed to go to *kepala lingkung's* house to listen to the sailors' stories about their journey.

When the children are from five to six years old, they participate in a variety of different tasks adjusted to their physical and mental maturity, such as fetching water and tending babies. "In this context, child care is, in parents' and childrens' own views, more a domestic task for children to learn than a specialized task of adulthood" (Weisner, 1987, p. 237). Boys and girls are given equal workloads and asked to do the same things, but when they are around ten to twelve years old, a modest gender role differentiation develops. During early years, however, personal qualities such as nurturance and compliance are equally valued in the behavior of boys and girls.

To understand Miang Tuu child development, we have to emphasize the household structure as an important element of the setting where the children learn about their roles and identities. The children learn about the sex roles their culture describes as proper by watching adult models.

In Miang Tuu two dyads are stressed above others: the mother–daughter and the mother–son. These are the lasting dyads through time and are the focal point in the mind of the villagers. Social status and position are related to family background and the economic situation. The child is soon aware of his position within the community hierarchy, and the way he acknowledges this will mold his attitudes toward himself and others.

The social differences between children are made explicit through the friendship of Leipi, *kepala's* son, and Halimu, son of a deceased member of *kapala's* crew. The boy's were always together. Halimu often lived with Leipi's family. They bought him clothes and brought him along as a playmate for Leipi on a voyage to Java, but Halimu was never treated as a son. His social status was clearly different and he certainly experienced the different status and role of higher and lower ranking villagers. Both boys recognized that in many aspects of daily village life the same rules did not apply to them both.

Also in the friendship between Owati (approximately eleven years old) and Yobaida (approximately nine) the different social status of the two girls appeared clearly. Owati was the privileged, self-confident "leader." Yobaida had to adjust to Owati's whims and often take over some chores of her friend. Owati is described as an intelligent and active child. She showed, however, signs of identity and role confusion related to female–male envy. This envy was expressed by her striving for a partial male role. But change occurred in her behavior, and she was able to outgrow this envy and obtain new means of narcissistic gratification by applying culturally accepted norms of female gender performances.

While Bonerate culture offers few sanctioned outlets for aggressive behavior, children's play with animals seems to provide an aggressive gratification to both the young "actors" and the adult onlookers. From approximately age four to age thirteen, children treat animals more and more roughly. After the approximate age of seven, girls take less direct part in cruelties toward animals than boys do. But like adults, girls love to watch the play. It is through a type of culturally constituted displacement of aggression that the Miang Tuu children's behavior toward animals can be best understood. Because of the cultural importance placed on nonviolent and nonaggressive cooperation within this small community, the Miang Tuuans have developed means to ban internal, intercommunity aggression.

Late childhood and early puberty is primarily treated within the frame of circumcision ceremonies in Chapter 4. Bonerate girls and boys are all circumcised. Anthropologists generally regard the major function of such initiation rituals as marking a change from child to adult status. How these rites are carried out and what their overt and symbolic contents are appear to depend on a variety of cultural and social factors. Although there certainly exist ritual means to mark a transition from childhood to adult status, I believe that we often have been too quick to interpret many initiation rituals as markers of such a transition. Psychologically a transition from childhood to adult status with the accompanying obligations can rarely happen overnight. It takes time to internalize a new status. Here, of course, the age of the initiates will be of crucial importance. Adulthood can be more than a matter of social recognition. To act like an adult one must be physically and psychologically ready for the prescribed behavior of that status. In the anthropological literature the status of youth (meaning no longer a child) seems at times to have been confused with an adult status.

Claiming that initiation rituals at Bonerate mark the change from child to adult status would not be empirically accurate. In Miang Tuu initiation marks several culturally important issues related to that transition, but the novices do not gain adult status at the completion of the circumcision ritual. Miang Tuu circumcisions are syncretistic in the sense that both Islamic and traditional elements are blended, and the ceremonies have multiple symbolic meanings. The rituals are public and have significance for the novices and other individuals as well as for village integration.

The circumcision of boys is now usually carried out at a hospital in Surabaya, Java, during a boy's first trip to sea as a member of a *perahu* crew. Consequently the boys are older than they used to be and no ceremonies or rituals are conducted. During the traditional circumcision rituals previously conducted in the village, boys were supposed to suppress pain. But the memory of blood and pain overshadowed all other memories of those who had passed the initiation. The ritual is interpreted as a possible expression of male envy of female reproduction. The traditional ritual did not place men ahead of women, but made them more equal. The abolition of male circumcision in Miang Tuu, if other major cultural changes do not follow, should not necessarily lead to role confusion among men or to a reduced male status, but rather to a growing male–female envy. It is not possible to verify if this is indeed true. The transition in male status from child to recognition as an adult seems now as before closely tied to the boy's achievements at sea.

Girls are usually "circumcised" some years earlier than boys—at an average age of eight years. The rituals last for two days during which all villagers are served food several times. A special costume is rented and a ritual leader is hired. The circumcision of girls is a symbolic act that consists of a light scratch with a bamboo knife at the inside of the upper thigh. There is neither pain nor blood; no risk to health is involved. Much ritual activity is conducted to ensure future fertility and to illustrate ideal female behavior.

Both the male and female ritual serve to strengthen sex-related self-identity among the novices. Among other things the rituals elaborate on the nature of being a man and a woman. This is important not only to the novices on the way to adulthood but also as a reminder to all villagers. Miang Tuu initiation rituals do not mark the transition from childhood to adult recognition, but confirm that the novices are on their way to adulthood. They obtain a formal lesson on some of the obligations that belong to adult status. They are not supposed to change overnight; initiation is merely a necessary step toward adulthood. Some childish behavior is supposed to be dropped after initiation. Girls should for instance be more *malu* when they wash themselves at the village wells or play on the beach. Both boys and girls should be more careful not to lose their temper and should restrain childish behavior from now on. Miang Tuu villagers' views on these matters are similar to Western ideas about this period of psychological transition:

> Just as we do not expect to wean a toddler overnight, we do not expect the adolescent to relinquish childhood without a struggle, without grief, without anxiety, without some relapse into the past. Success is gradual and fraught with relapse, trial and error. (Kaplan, 1985, p. 97)

A universal problem that must be solved in some way seems to appear at the time of adolescence. The problem is closely related to the constitution of personal identity. The question is how one perceives oneself as having continuity and sameness, despite changes in physical appearance and changes in felt expectations of behavior. How is an altered life situation best handled? In Western cultures many hold the view that adolescence is a lengthy period of inevitable psychological turmoil. Typical for this situation is a change from the feelings of love and desire for parents to hatred and compulsive disobedience. But even the most hostile adolescent boys or girls are unlikely to tolerate their destructive wishes regarding their parents or parent substitutes. Instead they fantasize that significant authority figures hate them or even are persecuting oppressors.

The title of Chapter 5, The Docile Time of Puberty and Adolescence, stresses the fact that, given a context and social structure other than that of modern Western cultures, adolescence need not be a stormy decade. This is not a particularly new observation, but in a cross-cultural perspective it is important to document the various ways that lead to a relatively smooth transition to adulthood. The present work is an effort in that direction. A seeming lack of opposition toward parents and village life does not necessarily imply that internal turmoil is absent. The crucial issue, then, is how Miang Tuu culture sets frames for acceptable behavior and at what costs the village youth internalize this cultural ideology. These are basic and difficult questions that I do not claim to have answered fully. During initiation rituals problematic issues of both personal and collective significance are in focus and at least some culturally acceptable solutions to the dilemmas are suggested. Many of these problems obviously have their roots in the socialization processes described in the first chapters. The young villagers strive to internalize their new identities, which include how to handle parental relations and how to relate to members of other generations and of the other sex. This must be managed within the terms set by Bonerate cultural ideology, which, when internalized, becomes the guardian of identity.

This is the period of the life cycle of Bonerate men and women when gender role expressions are most explicit. Both girls and boys become vain and narcissistic. Adolescent girls and boys mingle, but overt sexual passes seem absent. The boys appear to express an incestuous fixation on their mothers and sisters. Other village girls are at times referred to as sisters who should be protected from both physical and moral dangers. The adolescent boys are much concerned about their own virility as adult men and fear impotence. Although male youths express a wish to marry within the village, few get the opportunity. Insecurity in male role play is, among other factors, related to the lack of complete masculine role models within the village setting. It is argued that masculinity is demonstrated most explicitly outside the island when men are at sea and when they visit distant harbors. Both boys and girls seem to trust the advice of their parents and that of *kepala* and *ibu lingkung* about marriage. Still they were curious to learn about love marriages in Europe and wondered how that system could work. Adolescent boys show great devotion to their mothers—an emotional tie that seems to last through life. The father–son relationship is also close, but a mild avoidance is practiced in certain settings. Father and adolescent sons, for instance, seldom work closely together. According to the villagers this avoidance springs from the respect the son has for his father.

To the girls, the time of adolescence is somewhat different from that of their brothers. Girls easily move into adult work, whereas boys must push for permission to attempt many adult tasks. As the girl grows up, her gender identification is primarily achieved through her mother and other women in the village. There is no need for a dramatic alteration in mother–daughter relations because of an approaching marriage. The mother continues to be her confidante and ally, together with her sisters and other village girls her own age with whom she passed through initiation. In many traditional societies, the options for growing up into womanhood are prescribed and limited, and this sort of mother–daughter intimacy can pass as normal to themselves and to the other community members (Kaplan, 1985, p. 170). In Miang Tuu the mother–daughter dyad is a positively laden relationship and the focus of much village attention. The quality of this dyad inculcates the girl with a strong sense of gender role identity. Here feminine identification is based on the gradual way of becoming familiar with and obtaining increasing authority and responsibility over household management, exemplified by the person with whom the girl has been most involved since childhood.

Girls and boys do not give their parents a hard time as teenagers, neither do they detach from parental authority during adolescence. But the parents' experience of few conflicts with their adolescent children should not be interpreted to indicate that the transition from adolescence to adulthood occurs without psychological strain. That the youth feel pressures of moral and other obligations in their striving toward social maturity and recognition is documented in the descriptions of Haisa and Mellog, the adolescent girl and boy. In adolescence it is time to practice the emotional control ideals that were spelled out at the time of the puberty rites. To young women the emotional control requirements include shyness, chastity, and good-temperedness. Boys must keep their temper and ought to be polite. They too strive to conform in order to gain respect and recognition from the villagers. Adolescent boys appear insecure in their gender and age role performances. Whereas the boys who stay behind in the village long for the sea, they are not equally eager to leave their natal home at the prospect of marriage. Still, marriage is wanted and necessary to gain recognition as an adult. It is futile for most young men to invest their work on the swiddens or on modernization of their mothers' and sisters' homes in Miang Tuu, because these young men will spend their adult lives in other villages, in the home of their future wives. Their sisters remain in the village and carry out their adult life in familiar surroundings. Most adolescent boys become restless in Miang Tuu. They wait, pass the time, and often do not know what to do. They know they will be leaving the village and establishing obligations to people at other places. After they have left their natal home for marriage, they will return in the future as guests.

When I visited Bonerate in 1978, Miang Tuu was in many ways an isolated village. Community life flowed on much as it had done through the last four or five generations. Because the rate of modernization was still moderate, the villagers had time to adapt to the new sociocultural settings. The impact of new technology was indeed limited. The children did not attend schools, radios were few, and television had not been introduced.

Although I have not had the opportunity to revisit Bonerate, I know that many changes are likely to have taken place during the last eleven years or so. Today most children in Miang Tuu probably go to school, where they are exposed to socialization processes dramatically different from those at work in 1978. One could reasonably expect schooling to have consequences for not only the institutionalized child-tender practices, but also many other aspects of gender and role play. The grouping of pupils by age in the classroom would influence the composition of play groups, at least during school hours. Also, both legitimized ideals of competition and educational goals in the schoolroom setting, reinforced by an emphasis on *bahasa Indonesia* as the language of communication, are likely to lead to manifest changes in daily interaction among children and between children and adults. It would be interesting to investigate how these changes have influenced village interaction and how modernization processes have affected the identity formation of both young and older residents.

Many of the observations and analyses in this work would contribute significantly to our general understanding of socialization processes if a return visit to Bonerate were undertaken. Then one could show how changes in the social environment have influenced interactional patterns as well as the psychological constitution of the villagers.

I hope that the present book proves useful to those interested in socialization processes in a cross-cultural context. But my primary intention throughout has been to give an observer's account of what it was like to grow up in Miang Tuu in the late 1970s. I therefore have shown what options are chosen by young and older individuals in different situations and how Miang Tuu villagers describe appropriate behavior and feelings in a variety of particular circumstances.

Glossary

An asterisk indicates Bonerate words; the others are of Indonesian origin.

agar   seaweed
agar akar   black seaweed used as amulets
akar   root
*ama   father
anak   child
bahasa   language
Bajau   sea nomads, an ethnic group
bapak   father, older man
bapak lingkung   village, area chief
*batiranga   red mush made from leaves, possibly of henna
belanda   white people; Europeans, especially Dutch
bodoh   stupid, foolish
*bone   sand
Bonerate   island in the Flores Sea; name of a village; culture of Miang Tuu villagers
*bubu   fish weir
bubur   stew or soup
Bugis   ethnic group
bulan   month, moon
bulan sebelas   November, literally, the eleventh month
bundel   Dutch pillow
Butung   large island north of Bonerate
chamat   district officer
dingin   cold
gambus   stringed instrument, lute
Gerombola   gang, guerrilla
gila   crazy, stupid
gotong royong   mutual self-help, cooperative labor
gula   sugar, sweets, candy
ibu   mother
ibu kota   capital
ibu lingkung   wife of village or area leader
imam   Muslim religious leader
*ina   mother
joget   a dance
juragan   captain on a sailing ship
kabupatan   administrative area

kampung   village or section of a village
kapal   ship, boat
kemiri   oil or candle nut
kepala   head
kepala lingkung   village, area chief
kota   village, town
lambu   type of sailing ship
lingkung(an)   administrative area
lola   trochus snail
lombok   hot red pepper
malu   shy, respectful, modest, shameful, ashamed
massi   still
*****moane**   man, male
orang   person, people, man, woman
*****pakande**   food, a small meal
panas   warm, hot
*****pandita**   fish poison (priest in the Indonesian language)
parang   long-bladed bush knife
perahu   sailing ship
Ramadan   Muslim fasting month
rame   fun, lively, festive
*****rata**   flat
rupiah (Rp.)   the Indonesian currency
sakit   sick
sakit panas   sick with fever
sakit panas dingin   sick with malaria
sampan   small boat, dugout
sarong   loose skirt
Selayar   large island north of Bonerate
*****siri**   dignity
Surabaya   port town on eastern Java
syrikaya   fruit *(Annona squamosa)*
tape   drink of mildly fermented cassava
tikar   sleeping mat
Ujung Padang   port town and the administrative center of South Sulawesi
*****vovine**   woman, female

References

Ainsworth, Mary D. S. (1977). Attachment theory and its utility in cross-cultural research. In P. Herbert Leiderman, Steven R. Tulkin & Anne Rosenfeld (Eds.), *Culture and infancy: Variations in the human experience,* (pp. 49–67). New York: Academic Press.

Albert, Stuart, Amgott, Terry, Krakow, Mildred, & Marcus, Howard. (1979). Children's bedtime rituals: As a prototype of rite of safe passage. In *Journal of Psychological Anthropology, 2,* 87–105.

Barth, Fredrik. (1966). *Models of social organization.* Royal Anthropological Institute of Great Britain and Ireland, Occasional Papers, No. 23.

Berentzen, Sigurd. (1980). *Kjönnskontrasten i barns lek. En analyse av forholdet mellom begrepsdannelse og samhandling i en barnehage.* Bergen: Sosialantropologisk institutt, Universitetet i Bergen, Skriftserie No. 3.

Bettelheim, Bruno. (1962). *Symbolic wounds: Puberty rites and the envious male.* New York: Collier Books.

Bowlby, John. (1972). *Attachment and loss.* Vols. 1 and 2, Attachment. Hamondsworth: Pelican Books (reprint).

Brenner, Charles. (1974). *An elementary textbook of psychoanalysis* (Rev., expanded ed.). New York: Anchor Books.

Broch, Harald Beyer. (1981). Cultural variation on the islands in the Sea of Flores. *Archipel, 22,* 43–53.

Broch, Harald Beyer. (1983). The matrifocal warp of Bonerate culture. In B. Utas (Ed.), *Women in Islamic societies: Social attitudes and historical perspectives* (pp. 144–159). Scandinavian Institute of Asian Studies, Studies on Asian Topics No. 6. London: Curzon Press.

Broch, Harald Beyer. (1984). Bonerate. In R. V. Weekes (Ed.), *Muslim peoples: A world ethnographic survey* (pp. 169–172). Westport, Conn.: Greenwood Press.

Broch, Harald Beyer. (1985a). "Crazy women are performing in Sombali": A possession-trance ritual on Bonerate, Indonesia. *Ethos, 13* (3) 262–282.

Broch, Harald Beyer. (1985b). Resource utilization at Miang Tuu, a village on Bonerate island in the Flores Sea. *Contributions to Southeast Asian Ethnography* No. 4 (pp. 5–29).

Broch, Harald Beyer. (1987). Ethnic differentiation and integration: Aspects of interethnic relations at the village level on Bonerate. *Ethnic Groups, 7,* 19–37.

Broch, Harald Beyer. (1988). Between field and sea: The role of Miang Tuu women in village economy and society. In Jane Nadel-Klein & Dona Lee Davis (eds.), *To work and to weep. Women in fishing economies* (pp. 73–90). Social and Economic Papers No. 18 St. Johns, Institute of social and economic research, Memorial University of Newfoundland.

Brown, Judith K. (1963). A cross-cultural study of female initiation rites. *American Anthropologist, 65* (4) 837–853.

Brown, Judith K. (1973). The subsistence activities of women and the socialization of children. *Ethos, 1* (4) 413–423.

Burton, Roger & Whiting, John. (1963). The absent father and cross-sex identity. In R. E. Grinder (Ed.), *Studies in adolescence* (pp. 107–117). New York: MacMillan.

Casino, Eric S. (1976). *The Jama Mapun: A changing Samal society in the Southern Philippines.* Quezon City: Manila University Press.

Chin, S. C. (1977). Shifting cultivation: A need for greater understanding. *Sarawak Museum Journal, 25* (46) 107–128.

Chodorow, Nancy. (1974). Family structure and feminine personality. In Michelle Zimbalist Rosaldo & Louise Lamphere (Ed.), *Woman, culture and society (pp.* 43–66) Stanford: Stanford University Press.

Chodorow, Nancy. (1978). *The reproduction of mothering: Psychoanalysis and the sociology of gender.* Berkeley: University of California Press.

Conklin, Harold C. (1957). *Hanúnoo agriculture: A report on an integral system of shifting cultivation in the Philippines.* Rome: FAO Forestry Development Paper No. 12.

Dentan, Robert Knox. (1978). Notes on childhood in a nonviolent context: The Semai case (Malaysia). In Ashley Montagu (Ed.), *Learning non-aggression: The experience of non-literate societies* (pp. 94–143). New York: Oxford University Press.

Draper, Patricia. (1978). The learning environment for aggression and anti-social behavior among the !Kung. In Ashley Montagu (Ed.), *Learning non-aggression: The experience of non-literate societies.* New York: Oxford University Press.

Dussán de Reichel, Alicia. (1979). Child-rearing in a Colombian village. *International Social Science Journal, 31* (3).

Ember, Carol. (1973). Feminine task assignment and the social behavior of boys. *Ethos, 1* (4) 424–439.

Endicott, Kirk. (1979). *Batek Negrito religion.* Oxford: Clarendon Press.

Erikson, Erik. (1978). *Childhood and society.* St. Albans: Triad Paladin, Reprint.

Erikson, Erik. (1982). *The life cycle completed.* New York: Norton.

Flores, E. (1967). *Child rearing among a Moslem group in the Sulu Archipelago, Philippines.* Ann Arbor, Mich.: University Microfilms.

Freud, Anna. (1965). *Normality and pathology in childhood: Assessments of development. The Writings of Anna Freud,* Vol. 6. New York: International Universities Press.

Freud, Sigmund. (1961). *Beyond the pleasure principle.* New York: Norton.

Freud, Sigmund. (1974). *Sexuality and the psychology of love.* New York: Collier Books.

Fromm, Erich. (1970). The crisis of psychoanalysis [*Om Marx og Freud,* 1972]. Oslo: Pax Forlag.

Geertz, Hildred. (1974). The vocabulary of emotion: A study of Javanese socialization processes. In Robert A. LeVine (Ed.), *Culture and personality: Contemporary readings* (pp. 249–264). Chicago: Aldine. (Original work published 1959)

Goffman, Erving. (1959). *The Presentation of self in everyday life*. Garden City, N.Y.: Doubleday Anchor.

Honigmann, John J. (1967). *Personality in culture*. New York: Harper & Row.

Horney, Karen. (1973a). Premenstrual tension. In Karen Horney, *Feminine psychology*. New York: Norton.

Horney, Karen. (1973b). The dread of woman: Observations on a specific difference in the dread felt by men and women respectively for the opposite sex. In Karen Horney, *Feminine psychology*. New York: Norton.

Hsu, Francis L. K. (1972). Kinship and ways of life: An exploration. In Francis L. K. Hsu (Ed.), *Psychological anthropology* (pp. 509–567). Cambridge, Mass.: Schenkman.

Jacobsen, Adrian J. (1896). *Reise in die Inselwelt des Banda-Meeres*. Berlin: Verlag von Mitscher und Rostell.

Kagan, Jerome. (1977). The child in the family. *Daedalus, 106,* 33–56.

Kaplan, Louise. (1985). *Adolescence: The farewell to childhood*. New York: Simon & Schuster.

Klein, Melani. (1975). *The Psychoanalysis of children*. New York: Delta.

Koentjaraningrat. (1961). *Some social-anthropological observations on gotong rojong practices in two villages of central Java*. Ithaca: Cornell University, Modern Indonesia Project Series.

Koentjaraningrat. (1988). The Indonesian mentality and development. *Sojourn, 3* (2) 107–133.

Kriebel, D. J. S. (1920). Het Eiland Bonerate. *Bijdragen tot de Taal-, Land en Volkenkunde van Nederlandsch-Indie, 76,* 202–222.

La Fontaine, Jean. (1977). The power of rights. *Man, 12,* 421–437.

Le Bar, Frank. (Ed.) (1972). *Ethnic groups of insular Southeast Asia*. Vol. 1, Indonesia, Andaman Islands and Madagascar. New Haven: Human Relations Area Files Press.

LeVine, Robert A. (1977a). Parental goals: A cross-cultural view. In Hope Jensen Leichter (Ed.), *The family as educator* (pp. 52–65). New York: Teachers College Press.

LeVine, Robert A. (1977b). Child rearing as cultural adaptation. In P. Herbert Leiderman, S. R. Tulkin, & A. Rosenfeld (Eds.), *Culture and infancy: Variations in the human experience*. New York: Academic Press.

Levinson, David, & Malone, M. J. (1980). *Toward explaining human culture: A critical review of the findings of worldwide cross-cultural research*. New Haven: Human Relations Area Files Press.

Levy, Robert. (1978). *Tahitians: Mind and experience in the Society islands*. Chicago: University Press of Chicago.

Lundstrom-Burghoorn, Wil. (1981). *Minahasa civilization a tradition of change*. Gothenburg Studies in Social Anthropology, No. 2.

Maccoby, Eleanor. E. (1959). Role-taking in childhood and its consequences for social learning. *Child Development, 30,* 239–258.

Mattulada. (1982). South Sulawesi: Its ethnicity and way of life. *Southeast Asian Studies, 20* (1), 4–22.

Mead, Margaret. (1928). *Coming of age in Samoa*. New York: Dell.

Mead, Margaret. (1930). *Growing up in New Guinea*. New York: Morrow (1975).

Roberts, John M., Arth, Malcolm J., Bush, Robert R. (1959). Games in culture. *American Anthropologist, 61,* 597–605.

Rohner, Ronald P. (1975). *They love me, they love me not.* New Haven: Human Relations Area Files Press.

Rosaldo, Michelle Z. (1980). *Knowledge and passion: Ilongot notions of self and social life.* Cambridge: Cambridge University Press.

Saphir, E. (1932). Cultural anthropology and psychiatry. *Journal of Abnormal Social Psychology, 27,* 229–242.

Schwartzman, Helen B. (1978). *Transformations: The anthropology of children's play.* New York: Plenum Press.

Singer, Merrill. (1978). Pygmies and their dogs: A note on culturally constituted defense mechanism. *Ethos, 6* (4), 270–277.

Sorenson, Richard E. (1978). Cooperation among the Fore of New Guinea. In Ashley Montagu (Ed.), *Learning non-aggression: The experience of non-literate societies* (pp. 12–30). New York: Oxford University Press.

Spiro, Melford E. (1961). Social systems, personality and functional analysis. In Bert Kaplan (Ed.), *Studying personality cross-culturally* (pp. 93–127). New York: Row, Peterson.

Spiro, Melford E. (1965). Religious systems as culturally constituted defense mechanisms. In Melford E. Spiro (Ed.), *Context and meaning in cultural anthropology* (pp. 100–113). New York: The Free Press.

Spiro, Melford E. (1972). An overview and a suggested reorientation. In Francis L. K. Hsu (Ed.), *Psychological anthropology* (pp. 573–607). Cambridge, Mass.: Schenkman.

Spiro, Melford E. (1980). Culture and human nature. In George D. Spindler (Ed.), *The making of psychological anthropology* (331–360). Berkeley: University of California Press.

Super, Charles M. & Harkness, Sara. (1982). The development of affect in infancy and early childhood. In Daniel A. Wagner & Harold W. Stevenson (Eds.), *Cultural perspectives on child development* (pp. 1–19). San Francisco: W. H. Freeman.

Weisner, Thomas S. (1987). Socialization for parenthood in sibling caretaking societies. In J. B. Lancaster et al. (Eds.), *Parenting across the life span: Biosocial dimensions* (pp. 237–270). New York: Aldine De Gruyter.

Weisner, Thomas S., and Gallimore, Ronald. (1977). My brother's keeper: Child and sibling caretaking. *Current Anthropology, 18* (2), 169–191.

Whiting, Beatrice B. (1980). Culture and social behavior: A model for the development of social behavior. *Ethos, 8,* (2), 95–116.

Whiting, Beatrice B., & Whiting, John W. (1975). *Children of six cultures: A psycho-cultural analysis.* Cambridge, Mass.: Harvard University Press.

Whiting, John W., Kluckhon, R., & Anthony, A. (1958). The function of male initiation ceremonies at puberty. In Eleanor E. Maccoby et al. (Eds.), *Readings in social psychology* (pp. 359–370). (3rd. ed.). New York: Holt, Rinehart & Winston.

Winnicot, D. W. (1982). *Playing and reality.* Hammondsworth: Penguin Books.

Index

About the Author

HARALD BEYER BROCH is associate professor of anthropology at the Ethnographic Museum of the University of Oslo. He has studied the Hare Indian fur trappers of Northern Canada, and, as advisor to the Royal Norwegian Ministry of Development Corporation, has worked in several East African countries.

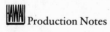Production Notes

This book was designed by Roger Eggers.
Composition and paging were done on the
Quadex Composing System and typesetting
on the Compugraphic 8400 by the design
and production staff of University of
Hawaii Press.

The text typeface is Sabon
and the display typeface is Gill Sans.

Offset presswork and binding were done by
Vail-Ballou Press, Inc. Text paper is
Writers RR Offset, basis 50.